BIRDS
OF
EDMONTON

ROBIN BOVEY
Illustrated by EWA PLUCIENNIK

LONE PINE

The Publishers:
Lone Pine Publishing
#206, 10426-81 Avenue
Edmonton, Alberta, Canada
T6E 1X5

Canadian Cataloguing in Publication Data

Bovey, Robin B. (Robin Bruce), 1947-
   Birds of Edmonton

   Includes index
   ISBN 0-919433-80-4

   1. Birds - Alberta - Edmonton. 2. Bird
watching - Alberta - Edmonton. I. Pluciennik,
Ewa, 1954-   II. Title
QL685.5.A4B692 1990   598.297123'34   C90-091161-1

Cover Design: Ewa Pluciennik
Colour Illustration: Ewa Pluciennik, Joan Johnston, Kitty Ho
Black and White Illustration: Donna McKinnon
Layout: Yuet Chan, Michael Hawkins, Beata Kurpinski
Printing: Kyodo Printing Co. (S'pore) Pte. Ltd., Singapore

Publisher's Acknowledgement
The publisher gratefully acknowledges the assistance of the Federal Department of Communications, Alberta Culture, the Canada Council, The Recreation, Parks and Wildlife Foundation, and the Alberta Foundation for the Literary Arts in the production of this book.

CONTENTS

PREFACE

Most of us have been intrigued by birds at one time or another. For some people this interest has evolved into a pastime, but for most of us it is a small facet of our lives that we enjoy when we can.

Many people have taken this further and enjoy feeding birds and having them around in the back yard. Birdwatching provides us with a tangible contact with nature in an urban existence. This book is for people who enjoy birds, but who don't necessarily regard themselves as expert birdwatchers, people who would like to know more, without buying comprehensive field guides and trying to decide which birds are actually found in the urban environment. It is a guide for the back yard birdwatcher.

Each bird is illustrated in colour, and there are descriptions and illustrations of the habitats within the City of Edmonton which are particularly attractive to birds. At the back of the book there is a section on how to attract birds to the yard. This section deals with feeders and nesting boxes, and explains which trees, shrubs and garden settings are most attractive to birds.

ACKNOWLEDGEMENTS

The book has been written very much as a cooperative venture and we are indebted to Wayne Campbell, Elizabeth John, Grant Kennedy, Kathie Kennedy, and Gerald McKeating for their help in preparing species descriptions and for their suggestions and encouragement. Thanks are owed also to Jim Butler of the University of Alberta, Jim Lange of the Edmonton Bird Club, Dave Elphinstone of Kinglet Natural History Services, and Cleve Wershler of Sweetgrass Consultants for providing expert advice and recommendations for revisions, and to Matt Fairbarns and E. Otto Hohn for consultations on the manuscript. Many thanks also to Joan Johnston, Kitty Ho and Donna McKinnon for assistance with the illustrations.

Robin Bovey
Ewa Pluciennik

BIRDS IN THE CITY

BIRDS PROVIDE a very real and tangible way of identifying with nature. Whether on a busy downtown city street or in a remote part of a national park, birds surround us and are comparatively easy to see and to appreciate — without the need for special knowledge or equipment. Over the last decade more and more people have taken up birdwatching in their spare time and today it is the fastest growing recreational activity in the western world. Whether actually going out on a hike to look for birds, or merely appreciating them as part of another recreational activity, bird-watching greatly enhances our appreciation for the environment and our enjoyment of the outdoors.

Most Albertans live in cities or towns, but this in no way diminishes the possibilities or the pleasures in looking for birds. Birds, like people, have adapted to the urban situation, and their variety and abundance in the city can be a constant source of fascination to anyone who cares to look. Many habitats in urban areas closely resemble natural habitats, and the limiting factors that most affect the presence of birds in the city are the pressures of human disturbance, and the availability of suitable nesting and feeding areas. Some of the more aggressive and common birds, such as the House Sparrow, European Starling, Black-billed Magpie, and Rock Dove (pigeon), have adapted so well to living alongside humans that they are often regarded as pests.

The back yard is one of the best places to watch birds; it provides people with a real opportunity to bring birds into their lives and to attract them out into the open. But it is by no means the only place in the Edmonton area to see birds. Some of the urban parks are truly natural areas and in these settings it is possible to see a wide variety of species that do not readily spring to mind as city birds — warblers, flycatchers, hawks, ducks and owls. These areas are waiting to be explored by anyone with the interest, time, and patience.

Some birds have been enticed into the city — perhaps the best example of this is the Peregrine Falcon, which normally chooses isolated nesting sites on cliff ledges. For the past few years, these rare falcons have been nesting in the centre of Edmonton, thanks to an enterprising scheme engineered by wildlife biologists. A pair of captive-bred birds were released onto a suitable nest site and they now return to their downtown summer location to breed every year, after wintering in Central America. They feed on the plentiful supply of pigeons, as well as many other species of birds found in and near our city.

It is quite possible to create suitable habitats for birds in the back yard, although wrens and chickadees are more likely to be attracted than falcons.

To fully appreciate the wealth of bird life in Edmonton, venture into some of the more natural areas of the urban environment. The birds that are to be found in the city are those which are looking for habitats similar to the natural areas outside the city, so choose the right habitats for the birds you hope to see, and the chances of a rewarding birdwatching sortie will be much improved.

Here in Alberta we live at the edge of the prairies, on the edge of the deciduous woodland, and of the coniferous forest. Choose to visit the urban equivalents of these habitats for the best bird-watching experiences.

The best tactic is to decide on a series of habitats to visit on an outing, and to go to areas where you know these habitats exist. Not surprisingly, the areas where there are mixtures of habitats will increase the likelihood of seeing birds. Wet areas and open water, surrounded by native trees, will provide some of the richest of urban birdwatching experiences.

Habitats

Within the city, there are many semi-natural and natural areas that are remnants of the unspoiled landscape that existed before human settlement increased to the extent that it has today. The more formal parks within the city are by no means natural to this part of Canada, but they provide birds and humans alike with areas that they can use and enjoy. The best spots for the birdwatcher are those that most closely resemble the natural areas of this province.

Grasslands

The prairie grasslands have all but gone now, replaced by the farmland that is so much a part of the Alberta landscape, and by our towns and cities. Nevertheless, there are areas of semi-natural grassland in the drier, south-facing parts of Edmonton's river valley and around the edges of the city. These are the areas over which the Red-tailed Hawk hunts, looking for small mammals, and where the American Goldfinch forages for seed. The introduced Gray Partridge also prefers this type of grassland, and small coveys of these birds will often explode into the air before gliding away and disappearing into the short grass cover again. In the winter, Snowy Owls and Snow Buntings forage over the frozen ground. This is not a habitat which teems with birds, unlike the deciduous woodland that readily invades the grassland, but it can provide worthwhile birdwatching expeditions.

Aspen Parkland

The aspen forest is an area much favoured by many bird species. It provides a wide variety of habitat types within the forest, with a dense understory of shrubs — many of which are very attractive to birds — such as the chokecherry, saskatoon berry, wild rose and gooseberry. In the riverine woodland bottoms of the river valleys, trees such as the balsam poplar are found, and at the edges of the river valley and on the southern valley slopes there are often drier open grassland areas. This is the prime city birdwatching habitat. Numerous species nest in the area: Black-capped Chickadees, Yellow Warblers, Black-billed Magpies, House Wrens, White-throated Sparrows, woodpeckers and some of the predatory birds such as Red-tailed Hawks and Great Horned Owls.

Try to choose the less disturbed areas of the aspen parkland in which to watch birds, as there will be a greater variety of birds in these areas and you may have the opportunity of seeing some of the more timid ones, such as the Pileated Woodpecker, which do not tolerate people's presence as well as many of the other species found in the city. In these areas, please stay on developed pathways so that you do not disturb the birds' natural habitat.

Coniferous Forest

The coniferous-dominated forest is typically found on the colder, north-facing slopes of the river valley where the climate is cooler and moister. The tree canopy is often denser here than in deciduous areas, so there is often less of a shrub layer, but plants such as bracted honeysuckle and black currant are typical. The bird life is less diverse in these areas than in other semi-natural habitats, and the birds are more difficult to see in the dense tree cover.

Wetlands

Any habitat where there is open water or even a damp marshy area is attractive to birds of all sorts. Some birds, such as ducks, feed and breed in these habitats, while others come to drink and bathe. The North Saskatchewan River, where it runs through the centre of the city, is perhaps the most obvious place to visit. Here you are likely to see gulls, ducks and even a Belted Kingfisher. There are also many other wetland habitats. Some, like the ponds in the city parks, are artificial, but so long as they have some surrounding vegetation and a semi-natural shore, birds will use them.

Willows often dominate the vegetation surrounding these areas, and a close look will reveal a variety of birds. One of the best wetland habitats is the slough, where there are likely to be Redwinged Blackbirds and many species of ducks in the reeds and cattails.

MILL CREEK RAVINE

The mix of coniferous and deciduous trees coupled with a streamside habitat attracts a wide variety of species to the ravine. Dense cover in the wilder sections provides nesting sites for some of the less common species.

HAWRELAK PARK

Several species of geese
and ducks use the pond
and marsh area of the park
as a stop-over during migration. A few nest on the island and
in adjacent woodlands. The open
area of the park is also an ideal location for sighting gulls and the occasional
large bird of prey. The woods near the river
are excellent locations for a good mix of
songbirds, such as Rose-breasted Grosbeaks,
Northern Orioles and Red-eyed Vireos.

PRAIRIE PARKLAND

This view from the south-east of
the city includes the open meadow
country beyond Millwoods.
Large-scale cultivation has lured
a large variety of prairie birds
further north. The mix of deciduous
trees in the parkland also provides
cover for species dependant
on woodland.

EDMONTON'S RIVER VALLEY

A great variety of birds nest in the diverse habitats of the river valley.

A birdwatching expedition along the riverbank in spring or summer should net over a dozen species sightings within an hour.

DOWNTOWN EDMONTON

Parks within the central core of the city have attracted some songbirds but crows, sparrows and pigeons — the urban scavenger birds — seem most abundant. Songbirds rarely nest in the smaller parks but use them as rest stops during migration.

BIRDS OF EDMONTON

KEY TO SYMBOLS

CONIFEROUS FOREST

GRASSLANDS & FIELDS

DECIDUOUS WOODLAND

WETLANDS

MIXED WOODS

MANICURED, RESIDENTIAL PARKS

RIVERINE WOODS

GARDENS & FEEDERS

RED-NECKED GREBE

Podiceps grisegena
crow-sized
Nests: May - June

THIS FEISTY looking bird, with its sharp tapered beak, is most likely to be seen in the city during spring and fall migration. It, along with the much smaller Horned Grebe, is a fairly common summer inhabitant of the larger ponds and shallow lakes of the province, many of which are found on urban outskirts.

Its nest of piled reeds is floating, anchored to living reed. The parents hunt insects, frogs, or small fish for the usual brood of four to five young. These, in turn, must be protected on their early forays from larger fish, especially northern pike.

Grebes patter along the water rapidly in their efforts to become airborne. Although usually silent, they keep cottagers awake with a sharp *kack* and enduring wail of courtship — reminiscent of a horse whinny — during late April and May, shortly after the ice has left the lakes.

Like other grebes, the Red-necked Grebe swallows feathers off the water. These are later regurgitated, and fish bones can be found in the feathery ball.

GREAT BLUE HERON

Ardea herodias
larger than gull-sized
Nests: April - May

THESE MAGNIFICENT, tall, great-winged birds arrive in this area in early April. They are likely to be seen in Edmonton only during migration or in late summer to early fall when the nesting colonies begin to disperse. At this latter stage they will make 50 kilometre round trips in the morning or evening for food.

Heronries, which are found at scattered points throughout central and north-east Alberta, are composed of bulky twig-and-reed nests often in bare, dead poplars. The copious amounts of white-wash produced by the nestlings can eventually lead to the deaths of trees. Nest sites must not be visited during the nesting season, as the birds are very shy and will desert their nests when disturbed in any way.

The great dark bird hunts in shallow water, walking slowly with head often atilt to spy small fish in striking distance. When alarmed it will squawk hoarsely. In flight, its S-shaped neck is a certain identifier. Often incorrectly referred to as a crane, the Great Blue Heron is not one: among other difference, cranes fly with their necks outstretched.

CANADA GOOSE

Branta canadensis
larger than gull-sized
Nests: April - May

IT IS A MAGNIFICENT bird, particularly the largest of the subspecies: and the largest are the most likely to be seen on the prairies of Western Canada. An almost assured sighting from mid-spring to early fall is along the highway between Edmonton and Calgary in a refuge and nesting site established to the west of the roadway a few miles south of Red Deer. Some birds winter on the open waters near the coal plant at Wabamun Lake, west of Edmonton.

The loyalty of mating pairs of Canada Geese has become the stuff of legend. Most ornithologists agree that a pair will mate for life. On the death of one, the surviving mate may remain solitary.

Canada Geese are impressively adaptable in seeking nesting sites. In the wild they will nest on the ground, on an island or even in the abandoned nest of a large bird. They also quickly recognize the consideration of farmers who drop bales of hay or straw in the centre of a slough to create a nesting platform. During the nesting season the gander patrols the environs of the nest and attacks intruders with savage pecks and its powerful wings. Unlike most ducks, geese are as much at home on land as they are on the water.

GREEN-WINGED TEAL

Anas crecca
smaller than crow-sized
Nests: May

THE GREEN-WINGED TEAL is one of Alberta's smallest ducks, and it chooses its habitat to suit its size. Tiny ponds, small potholes and roadside ditches all seem appropriate to its needs. As the teal is a dabbling duck, the shallow water is ideal for its tip-up feeding method.

The nesting pair will mate in mid-spring when ice is still on the larger lakes. They seem content with very small bodies of water and may experiment with a back yard lily pond, but a roadside ditch is a far more likely permanent choice.

The nest will be near the water in a depression lined with down and grass. Ten or more dirty white eggs will be laid. The Blue-winged Teal, a similar but very slightly larger bird, is more likely to nest in larger marshes.

Look for the Green-winged Teal between April and November.

MALLARD
Anas platyrhynchos
gull-sized
Nests: May - June

THE MALLARD is perhaps the most common and the best known of all the city's ducks. It readily adapts to people and can become quite tame in urban parks.

Mallards are dabbling ducks and, when feeding, they often upend to reach further below the surface. They feed on a wide variety of food, from water weeds and other vegetation, to seed and grain, to small insects. They usually arrive in their nesting areas in the spring just as the ice is breaking up. During the mating season, the female is pursued by numerous suitors.

They nest near water and the more drably coloured female does most of the incubating, where she is well camouflaged on the nest. Once the young hatch, the female leads her young to the nearest water and in the city this sometimes involves a journey through the streets.

Although many Mallards fly south in the fall to avoid freeze up, some birds remain and take advantage of sewage outfalls which keep the water open. In winter, Mallards are most often seen on the river downstream of the city centre. Look for them in Gold Bar Park.

COMMON GOLDENEYE

Bucephala clangula
crow-sized
Nests: May

THE GOLDENEYE is a diving duck, and its habitat is restricted to rivers, lakes and large ponds. It is likely to be seen in the city during migration, but it will remain in the fall and even throughout the winter, so long as open water is available. Look for Common Goldeneyes in winter downstream of Edmonton's city centre.

The Common Goldeneye depends on trees for its nesting site and requires a cavity with at least a ten centimetre opening. The female usually seeks out the empty nest hole of a Pileated Woodpecker but may try any large hole such as a sagging stove-pipe, shattered tree stump or hollow swag that promises to protect her eight to fifteen greenish-white eggs. (Buffleheads and Wood Ducks also seek out woodpecker holes as nesting sites.)

The female Common Goldeneye has a strong sense of territory and protects both her area of water and her nesting site from all but the mate she has selected. The voice of the female is a muted *wook*, while the male shrills a rising whistle. The male's wingbeat also produces a whistle.

BUFFLEHEAD

Bucephala albeola
smaller than crow-sized
Nests: June

THIS IS A SMALL DUCK. The male is black and white with a large wedge of white on the side of its head, while the female is predominantly brown. Buffleheads arrive in Alberta as soon as the ice melts from the lakes, and breed on ponds and lakes in or near open woodland. After mating, the female leaves the pond and searches for a nearby tree cavity, often an old flicker nest. It has been shown that the density of Buffleheads in an area varies with the availability of abandoned woodpecker nests. They show a nesting preference for beaver ponds and quiet, undisturbed areas.

The female lays a clutch of eggs which are incubated for 29 to 31 days. On hatching, the young tumble out of the nest and follow their mother to the nearby pond or lake. They can swim and dive immediately, and remain on the pond until they can fly at seven or eight weeks of age.

The Bufflehead eats aquatic invertebrates. In fall, Buffleheads gather into groups before beginning their southerly migration.

COMMON MERGANSER

Mergus merganser
larger than gull-sized
Nests: June

ALTHOUGH MALE common mergansers have green heads, as do male Mallards, the two species are not easily confused. The Common Merganser is larger, longer and more slender in profile, with a characteristic long thin red bill and pure white breast and sides. The female has a brown head with conspicuous crest, white breast and greyish back.

Its beak is finely toothed, which enables it to catch and hold its prey of fish. It catches fish that are the right size to swallow whole, since it is unable to tear fish apart. Mergansers nest on the ground — usually under an upturned tree root, an old log, or even a dense bush. When the young hatch, they are taken to water and fed on small fish and other suitably-sized prey items.

Common Mergansers rarely overwinter in Edmonton, although a pair is often seen on the open water at Wabamun Lake. Fishing is difficult for the birds when much of the water is frozen over; they have to swim under the ice in pursuit of fish. They swim very fast on these forays and frequently cover considerable distances underwater. Look for them on the North Saskatchewan River in April and May.

Inset: *female*

27

BALD EAGLE

Haliaeetus leucocephalus
larger than gull-sized
Nests: northern lakes and in the mountains

THE BALD EAGLE, the national emblem of the United States of America, is in fact far more numerous in Canada. During most of the year it is found near water and, when it wants to, is adept at catching fish — which it plucks from just below the surface with its talons. Much more frequently, it feeds on carrion that it finds on the shore or floating in the water. It frequently steals food from Ospreys, expert fishers, by diving at them and chasing them until they drop their fish. The Bald Eagle often catches the fish before it hits the water.

Bald Eagles build huge nests in trees and will often reuse a nest year after year, the nest eventually reaching an immense size.

Watch for Bald Eagles in and around Edmonton, particularly in the river valley, from late March to mid-April, and again from October to mid-November. They are never numerous but they sometimes rest on an old tree beside the river, or soar high above the river valley. When migrating back through our city in the late fall, they rely quite heavily on ducks for prey. In mild winters, the occasional bird remains late along the river, feeding on whatever it can catch or find to eat.

SHARP-SHINNED HAWK

Accipiter striatus
larger than robin-sized
Nests: May - June

THESE SMALL hawks are wonderfully equipped as woodland predators, with short cupped wings to allow them swift manoeuverability in their determined chase after small birds, squirrels, bats and, occasionally, large insects.

Sharp-shinned Hawks are most likely to be seen in the river valley or in the clearings of heavily wooded parkland, usually between April and October. The best time to look for them is from August to mid-September, when Sharp-shins follow the passerine migration. At this time, you will often see them soar.

The preferred nesting site is a large tree, often a conifer, where the pair will build a large, flat platform of twigs and bark. Smaller twigs on the bottom often indicate that the nest of some other large bird has been usurped.

Three to five bluish, spotted eggs will yield young before summer, and fledglings which are already hunting by late August. A high-pitched *ke-ke-ke-ke* of nervous adults may reveal the nest location.

The Cooper's Hawk, a larger, crow-sized bird, is also occasionally seen around Edmonton. Its tail is more rounded than is that of the Sharp-shinned Hawk.

RED-TAILED HAWK

Buteo jamaicensis
larger than crow-sized
Nests: April - May

A DARK BAND ACROSS the chest together with its lighter belly will identify this splendid bird, as the tail does not turn completely red until the bird's fourth or fifth year. The Red-tailed Hawk is seen quite frequently from April to October, using the uplift currents of south-facing hills as it soars effortlessly along Edmonton's river valley.

Nests are commonly located in the higher branches of large poplar trees, or occasionally nest on cliff faces. The large stick nest will contain a central cup in which one to four whitish faintly marbled eggs are laid.

The pair mates for life and each spring the male and female engage in a courtship flight that will take them high above the earth, only to plunge down to treetop level and begin the display once more.

Red-tailed Hawks seem to prefer open parkland for hunting and will perch on fence-posts along the roadway until a vehicle stops nearby. The call is a harsh descending scream: *kee-aheerr*.

The closely related Rough-legged Hawk, which lacks the red tail, may be seen in fields on the city's outskirts from late fall to early spring, and Swainson's Hawks — which have a red-brown bib — are often seen on the perimeters of the municipal airport and on Highway 14 south of the Sherwood Park turnoff.

AMERICAN KESTREL

Falco sparverius
smaller than robin-sized
Nests: May - June

THIS MINIATURE, jay-sized falcon is sometimes confused with its slightly larger cousin, the Merlin. The males of both species have blue wing tops and brownish underparts but the American Kestrel has a reddish-brown back, and black and white face markings.

American Kestrels prefer the edges of woods and farm fields, and will nest along the river. The males are the first to arrive in spring, usually in mid-April; females follow a week or two later to be offered a tree cavity, a woodpecker nesting box, a gap in a derelict wall, or a crumbling magpie nest. The choice seems to be limited only by the male's imagination and the female's acceptance. Four or six creamy, brown-blotched eggs are laid in the cavity without benefit of nest-lining. When fledged, the young stay with the family group and can be seen on telephone wires, fence posts and light standards. The birds migrate south in September.

Large insects and mice are the usual prey. The American Kestrel characteristically hovers while hunting, waiting for movement before it swoops to the ground. Its call is frequent, a rapid *killy-killy-killy*.

MERLIN

Falco columbarius
larger than robin-sized
Nests: May

YEAR-ROUND residents of ed-monton, Merlins are small falcons which were once known as Pigeon Hawks. They are more common than Peregrine Falcons, and are smaller and lacking the black "moustache." However, both falcons share the general body outline and pointed wings. The flight of Merlins is rapid and direct; they may soar, but they do not hover.

Their prey includes smaller birds and large insects such as grasshoppers. Merlins can be commonly seen hunting Bohemian Waxwings in the winter in urban areas, as they dive into a resting flock, catching stragglers among the surprised birds. They also hunt by chasing a small bird high into the sky and catching it as it tries to descend.

Merlins nest in tall trees, favouring spruce trees in the city and using the abandoned nests of large birds such as magpies or crows. As few as two and occasionally as many as seven, but usually four or five, eggs are laid.

PEREGRINE FALCON

Falco peregrinus
crow-sized
Nests: May - June

THE PEREGRINE FALCON does not immediately spring to mind as an urban bird, but it can now be sighted in downtown Edmonton, and in Calgary as well. In recent years many Peregrine Falcons have died from pesticide poisonings in their wintering grounds in Central and South America, and the birds were brought into our city as part of a reintroduction program, in an attempt to increase numbers of these exciting falcons in Alberta.

They nest on the ledges of office blocks; this suits them well as it approximates a natural nest site of a ledge on a high cliff. Edmonton's Peregrine Falcons feed on the numerous downtown pigeons, and those who witness an aerial chase will begin to appreciate why they were so prized by medieval falconers. Nevertheless, they are now rare in the province and you should count yourself fortunate to see one. They are similar in appearance to the smaller, more common, Merlin.

GRAY PARTRIDGE
Perdix perdix
crow-sized
Nests: June

IMPORTED FROM HUNGARY and released south of Calgary in 1908, this smallest of Alberta's game birds has thrived in open country. Although its breast, back and sides are bluish-grey, it has a tan face and throat which distinguish it from the larger bush-dwelling Ruffed Grouse and Sharp-tailed Grouse. A conspicuous reddish mark on the chest is diagnostic, and its call is a loud *girr-hak*.

Gray Partridges prefer the open fields, and can be seen in flocks in winter on city outskirts and the edges of our parks. They sustain themselves on grain in stubble and low ditches, and use farms for protection. When flushed, the sudden cackle of a dozen partridges can be startling to a cross-country skier.

Hens nest in May and June in ditch areas or beside low brush in a grass-lined depression. Both parents raise the ten to fifteen chicks.

Although Gray Partridges are now well-established throughout the year in Alberta, particularly in the open southern half, their numbers are often sharply reduced in a severe winter.

RING-NECKED PHEASANT

Phasianus colchicus
larger than gull-sized
Nests: May - June

THE MALE ring-necked pheasant is a spectacular bird with a brilliant green head with a red face patch above a white collar. Both male and female have long, tapering tails. The female can be distinguished from the Sharp-tailed Grouse by its dark spotting and general brownish appearance, and the absence of white in the plumage.

Ring-necked Pheasants occasionally make their way into urban back yards and city parks. They can often be found in brushy areas along the sides of some city ravines, such as the McKenzie and McKinnon ravines. They have been introduced from Asia to the grain-belt areas of Alberta, from irrigated lands in the south to open-field habitat in the Peace River country. Severe winters have periodically reduced populations to only isolated numbers.

The bird, particularly the cock, is quite visibly an exotic in Alberta. It gathers a harem of perhaps six hens which nest in leaf or grass-lined depressions on brush edges, cattail clumps or open fields. Ring-necked Pheasants are year-round residents of this province.

RUFFED GROUSE

Bonasa umbellus
gull-sized
Nests: May

THEY EVOKE THE SOLITUDE of the woodlands with a muffled, distant drumming that the ear, at first, isn't sure it has heard. Minutes later the slow thumping begins again, drums, and is lost in beats too rapid to distinguish.

The solitary male is perched solidly on a fallen log — its ruffed neck stretched and its fan tail extended — beating cupped wings against its sides. It will be preoccupied with its courting, and can be discovered and watched if the listener's approach is slow and noiseless. The male's drumming is usually heard in spring, but can sometimes be heard again in late summer or fall.

Ruffed Grouse usually make their way into Edmonton through the river valley, although some fly into perimeter suburbs from adjacent woodlands. Look for them in thick brush along the river, or in ravines. Most of those found in Alberta are of the gray race, although a few individuals resemble the reddish subspecies of the south and east and southwest British Columbia.

Females build a rough nest of leaves and grass protected by a fallen tree and lay seven to thirteen buff-coloured eggs. Ruffed Grouse are residents of Edmonton throughout the year.

AMERICAN COOT

Fulica americana
smaller than crow-sized
Nests: May - June

A WESTERN NAME for the coot is "Mudhen," a nickname which aptly describes its characteristic behaviour. It is a common water bird in this area between April and October, and can often be seen walking about on the mud around the edges of ponds.

American Coots feed by diving for aquatic vegetation and some invertebrates. They also feed along the edges of ponds and sloughs, where they hunt for insects and snails. They build a floating nest of reeds and rushes in the vegetation at the edge of the water and lay five to eight eggs.

Once migration starts in the fall, large numbers of coots congregate, and on occasion hundreds will seem to fill a small pond completely. Except when migrating, coots rarely fly and offer the hunter little sport: real sitting ducks.

KILLDEER
Charadrius vociferus
robin-sized
Nests: May - June

THE KILLDEER'S Latin name *vociferus* is no misnomer: the bird announces its presence with its shrill and persistent call, *dee-dee-dee* or *kill-dee*, after which it is named. It is a large plover and is easily recognized by its two black breast bands. The orange-brown rump is also distinctive. It is most commonly seen in Edmonton between April and September. Killdeer feed around the edges of ponds and lakes and, after nesting, are often seen on lawns or in open parks.

Feigning injury is the Killdeer's most notable talent. It makes an elaborate effort to lure intruders away from its nest with a "distraction display." It feigns a broken wing, sometimes a broken leg as well, as it scuttles and flaps along the ground away from its nest. It may even fake a return to a non-existent nest where it will fluff itself and settle down in hopes of luring the pursuer farther afield.

Despite these performances, the Killdeer is not a particularly wary bird. It often nests within the city, in marshy areas or on the river's gravel bars, and often a considerable distance from water — in railway yards, pastures or even on golf courses. The nest is a small depression or scrape on ground or gravel, with four buff and spotted eggs accompanied by a few pebbles.

SPOTTED SANDPIPER

Actitis macularia
smaller than robin-sized
Nests: May - June

THESE CAN BE regularly seen on the river banks from May through early September, teetering along the shoreline. The birds seem unconcerned until approached too closely and then will fly out in a low arc over the water to return to the shoreline further along. They are readily identified in flight by the stiff vibration of downward-pointing wings as they soar between rapid wing beats.

The flesh-coloured or yellowish legs of the Spotted Sandpiper are almost blurred by its sudden dashes along the shore. It seems to bob almost continuously on its long legs as it searches among the sand, stones and tufts of grass for insects.

Its nest is normally very close to water and is a depression in the ground, lined with grass, small leaves or moss. Four greenish, brown or pinkish-buff eggs with brown splotches will hatch before summer to allow the chicks to develop before an early migration south.

The voice of the Spotted Sandpiper, although not as distinctive as its vibrating wings in flight and its restless bobbing walk, is a sharp *peet-weet* or *weet-weet* in series.

COMMON SNIPE

Gallinago gallinago
larger than robin-sized
Nests: June

THIS SHORE BIRD IS often solitary and usually still when seen along the margin of a pond, slough or riverbank. Its long, straight beak (the length of a small finger) and striped head identify it on the ground. Once airborne, it has a distinctive zig-zag pattern of flight which will confirm the sighting.

The Common Snipe, resident in Calgary between April and October (and occasionally until December), feeds by probing deeply into the mud in search of worms and other small animals. The tip of its beak is both flexible and sensitive.

When flushed it screeches a harsh *zhek* and moves off rapidly in erratic flight. During spring courtship the flying male produces a hollow *oo-oo-oo* sound with his stiffly spread tail feathers.

The female nests in a grass-lined depression hidden by vegetation. The usual four eggs are olive-brown and darkly mottled.

FRANKLIN'S GULL

Larus pipixcan
smaller than crow-sized
Nests: May - June

A SMALL GULL with white underparts and a black head, the Franklin's Gull is common throughout the prairies, and is likely to be seen in flocks. These gulls can be seen following a plow in late spring, looking for worms and dead mice, or hawking for insects. Their enthusiasm for grasshoppers in the fall has earned them the plaudits of farmers for decades.

Large colonies of the birds can number up to 40,000. They will return to the same site and nest on piled reeds floating in shallow water. The usual three eggs are brownish-buff.

They are most likely to be seen in the city during spring and fall migrations, again in large flocks. Smaller colonies will nest in larger ponds on the outskirts.

The voice of the Franklin's Gull is a nasal *kuk kuk kuk*.

BONAPARTE'S GULL

Larus philadelphia
smaller than crow-sized
Nests: May - June

IN ALBERTA, if the head of a bird is black and it has a white triangle from the forward bend of the wing to its tip, it's almost certainly a Bonaparte's Gull. The black bill of this summer visitor to Edmonton will help to make definite identification. The only serious alternative is the black-headed Franklin's Gull, which has dark wing tips and a reddish beak.

The Bonaparte's Gull is normally seen near water and is quite common in the river valley. During its nesting period — which takes place primarily in the boreal forest region of the province — it is likely to be found in the upper branches of a spruce tree. Its twig-and-grass nest will hold two or three olive, dark-blotched eggs.

The Bonaparte's Gull is more dainty and tern-like than other gulls in Alberta. Its call is a low, nasal, tern-like *cher*. Its name commemorates Prince Lucien Bonaparte, a nephew of the Emperor Napoleon, who visited North America in his travels and first described this gull.

RING-BILLED GULL

Larus delawarensis
larger than crow-sized
Nests: May - June

THESE ARE THE COMMON scavenging gulls of the city, seen in Edmonton between March and November. They nest beyond the outskirts, preferably in island colonies, but can be seen on its daily commuter runs to dumps, supermarket parking lots and school yards. This pattern begins in early spring and continues to late fall, with the brownish young joining the daily flight by late summer.

With nesting behind them, Ring-billed Gulls began to flock at more convenient resting sites, particularly along the river. Their flights over the city lower, closer to the treetops in the fall. When landed, they are reluctant to move aside for shoppers or parking automobiles.

Adult Ring-bills are readily identified by a black band which encircles the beak just before its sharp tip. Their call is a squealed *ky-eew*.

ROCK DOVE

Columba livia
smaller than crow-sized
Nests: Year round

MORE COMMONLY known as a pigeon, this year-round resident is not native to North America. It originally came from the Mediterranean, but has since been introduced into various parts of the world. Once used as a domestic food source, the Rock Dove is now more particularly used for pigeon racing. It has adapted well to inner city living and the ledges of buildings provide a good substitute for its more natural habitat of rocky cliffs.

The birds make a scant nest on a ledge and produce several broods each year, sometimes nesting even in winter. The young are fed on "pigeon milk" to start with — a liquid produced in the crop of the adult from predigested food. Pigeons can become urban pests, as their excrement builds up on the ledges of the buildings on which they breed and roost. Those of downtown Edmonton have to contend with a very efficient predator in the Peregrine Falcon, which regularly feeds on Rock Doves while nesting in the city.

GREAT HORNED OWL

Bubo virginianus
smaller than gull-sized
Nests: March - April

ALBERTA'S PROVINCIAL BIRD haunts the ravines of the river valley, moving almost soundlessly in its late evening and night-long hunts. The prey is quite often a striped skunk, a bird, a rabbit or a ground squirrel. Even an intruding human is not immune to its long talons in early spring, when a nesting pair selects an old hawk or crow's nest, or possibly a hollow tree, and begins the defence of its territory. Although the Great Horned Owl normally attacks only when its nest tree is climbed, it is wise to keep your distance.

The pair usually starts nesting in late February. It will produce two or three large white eggs, protect them and the chicks through-out spring and summer, and urge the young birds to move off to new territory in the fall.

Although seen only occasionally, either at dusk or when roosting in large trees during the day, the Great Horned Owl can often be heard in the river valley in early spring. You may occasionally locate its roost during the day as it is being harras-sed by a flock of crows or magpies. Its deep-throated *whoo-hoo-hoo*, resonating out of the dark, prickles the scalp of even the most experienced of bird watchers.

SNOWY OWL

Nyctea scandiaca
larger than gull-sized
Nests in the Arctic

THE SNOWY OWL IS a winter visitor to Alberta. It breeds in the tundra regions of the Arctic where it lays eggs in a grass-lined depression on the ground. It is a circumpolar species, being distributed all around the north pole. In the Arctic it feeds on lemmings and other small mammals. Some individual Snowy Owls come south to Alberta every year; others remain in the north. Every number of years an explosion of their population occurs here: this phenomenon may be related to food abundance.

Snowy Owls can be seen in the prairies from November to late March. They occupy territories in open areas such as ploughed fields, and choose perches within the territory where they are often visible. They can commonly be seen sitting on telephone poles along the highways. Snowy Owls hunt during the daytime by flying slowly and noiselessly over fields, and dropping suddenly on mice and voles. Both eyes and ears are used in hunting. Banding studies show that these owls often return to the same winter territory year after year.

This bird is well adapted to life in the cold, having a thick feather coat which almost hides its bill, and even feathered legs.

NORTHERN SAW-WHET OWL

Aegolius acadicus
larger than sparrow-sized
Nests: May - June

THIS SMALL brown nocturnal owl is a year-round resident of Edmonton. It is quite confiding, and once located can be watched for a long time. Look for it roosting in the branches of a conifer tree during the day. If a group of smaller birds see an owl, they often spend minutes scolding the bird vociferously, so it is often worth investigating a loud commotion in the trees. This owl gets its odd name from one of its calls, a high pitched *kee-kee-kee-kee* that sounds like someone using a rasp on a saw to sharpen it. Listen for this call in April and May in wooded areas of the city, as this is when the male owls set up their territories. Northern Saw-whet Owls nest in the old nest holes of woodpeckers, and will use nest boxes of a suitable size set against the trunks of larger trees. The owls hunt by night for small rodents and will occasionally catch small birds and even bats.

Look, too, for the larger Short-eared Owls which overwinter in Edmonton, particularly in the open country in the Mill Woods area.

RUBY-THROATED HUMMINGBIRD

Archilochus colubris
smaller than sparrow-sized
Nests: June

THE RUBY-THROATED Hummingbird is the only hummingbird likely to occur in Edmonton gardens. It is more inclined to be mistaken for a large insect, such as a hawkmoth, than for any other bird. It obtains most of its nourishment from flowers, and many tubular flowers have evolved for pollination by the hummingbird. These provide a high nectar "reward," and hummingbirds will visit not only red flowers, but also red-mouthed feeders, and even red clothing and other red items.

Hummingbirds use a lot of energy as they dart rapidly from flower to flower, and supplement their nectar diet with small insects and tree sap, following Sapsuckers to obtain the latter. They require up to 50% of their body weight in food daily and to save energy they enter a state of torper, or low energy consumption, at night. The hum for which they are named results from the rapid beating of the wings.

Hummingbird habitats include gardens and woodland edges. Their nests are wonderful structures. Less than 4 cm in diameter, they are made from lichens, mosses and plant down, and held together with spider webs. Two eggs, white and rather large considering the size of the bird, are laid.

The Ruby-throated Hummingbird can be seen in Alberta from mid-May to September or early October.

BELTED KINGFISHER

Ceryle alcyon
larger than robin-sized
Nests: June

BELTED KINGFISHERS FEED on a variety of aquatic foods — fish, frogs, tadpoles and insects. To see them, look near open water, from the river valley to smaller ponds. They like to fish from a perch overhanging the water, where they can see their prey moving below. The Belted Kingfisher is the only blue bird that fishes by diving into the water. It has a long black bill and a very distinctive crest, and its rattling call is a good clue to its presence.

Kingfishers seek out holes in riverbanks and make their nests at the ends of the burrows. Like those of many hole-nesting birds, the eggs are white. Kingfisher nest holes are particularly smelly once the eggs have hatched and the parents have started bringing back fish to the young.

Although a few Belted Kingfishers may overwinter where there is open water, most arrive in Alberta once the river and pond ice has broken up, and migrate south as soon as freeze-up starts.

YELLOW-BELLIED SAPSUCKER

Sphyrapicus varius
smaller than robin-sized
Nests: May - June

POPLARS AND BIRCHES PROVIDE a major food source for sapsuckers. They supply both insects and a sweet sap for these unobtrusive woodpeckers, which are most likely to be seen in river valley areas of the city or in large wooded parks. The bird is decidedly noisy in spring when its sharp, stacatto rapping can waken nearby residents. Communication is achieved by tapping in a broken series on a dry tree trunk. In an earlier time, when metal chimneys were the norm, Yellow-bellied Sapsuckers would use the resounding stove pipes to declare territory and announce a mating disposition.

The Yellow-bellied Sapsucker also taps in pursuit of food, creating rows of small holes through the bark of deciduous trees, particularly birch, to reach the sap layer beneath. It will return to this cluster of holes after the sap has filled them, to eat both the sap and insects which have accumulated.

The Yellow-bellied Sapsucker can be found in our wooded areas and treed river valleys from May to September. While walking through aspen woods in mid-June, listen for the steady calls for food from the young. This is an easy way of finding sapsucker nest cavities.

DOWNY WOODPECKER

Picoides pubescens
smaller than robin-sized
Nests: May - June

THE DOWNY WOODPECKER is a permanent resident in Alberta and can easily be attracted to gardens in the winter by offerings of suet or crushed nuts. It is similar in appearance to the Hairy Woodpecker, although smaller (18 cm long as opposed to 23 cm for the Hairy Woodpecker). Its beak length, which is half the length of its head, is shorter in proportion to the head than is that of the Hairy Woodpecker.

In the spring, territoriality is announced by rapid drumming on dead wood. Areas containing deciduous trees are preferred to coniferous stands. A new nesting hole is excavated annually in a tree trunk, with an entrance only two or three centimetres in diameter. Both parents share the duties of feeding the young; during this time, nest holes are fairly easy to locate as the young are noisy when the adults alight with food. During the winter, the birds are fairly approachable as they search for food in cracks of bark.

The Downy Woodpecker's call is distinctive: a rapid whinny descending in pitch.

HAIRY WOODPECKER

Picoides villosus
larger than sparrow-sized
Nests: May

ITS DISPROPORTIONATELY large bill and larger size will distinguish this white-backed woodpecker from its cousin the Downy Woodpecker. Both year-round residents are most visible in the Edmonton area during winter, but in spring the Hairy Woodpecker tends to nest in deep woods, further from human habitation. It will only rarely come to a feeder for suet, although a few have chosen to take up residence in suitable birdhouses.

The customary nesting site is a previously used or newly excavated cavity in a decaying spruce or poplar. From three to six white eggs are laid on wood chips.

Hairy Woodpeckers are credited with a remarkable ability to locate insect grubs in old or rotting trees. They tap gently at first, then hammer swiftly through to extract the grub with a long, sticky and barbed tongue.

The call is a loud and sharp *peeck*, sharper in pitch than is that of the Downy Woodpecker.

NORTHERN FLICKER

Colaptes auratus
larger than robin-sized
Nests: May

THERE ARE TWO SUBSPECIES of the Northern Flicker seen in Edmonton, the yellow-shafted and the red-shafted, although the red-shafted is uncommon here as it has a more western distribution. The two have very similar colouration patterns when sitting; their identifying colours are prominently displayed under the wings so that they are noticeable only when the birds are in flight. When identifying a flicker which is perched, look for a black moustache on the yellow-shafted male, a red moustache on the red-shafted male. To confuse the issue, a red patch at the back of the neck identifies either a male or female Yellow-shafted Flicker. This situation is further complicated by the fact that the two races freely hybridize, producing intermediate plumage characteristics in some birds.

Northern Flickers are comparatively easy to identify in flight. They fly in a series of swoops with rapid wing beats at the top of each curving glide. The call is an easily recognized *wick-wick-wick*.

Usually present in Edmonton only between May and October, although a few will overwinter, Northern Flickers will nest in an urban environment if there is sufficient space around them. A standard woodpecker box attached to a tree may prove successful. (See birdhouse section in latter part of the book.)

PILEATED WOODPECKER

Dryocopus pileatus
larger than crow-sized
Nests: May

THIS LARGEST remaining woodpecker in North America is the size of a crow and dull black in appearance except for a scarlet crown, crest and moustache. A white line below its eye extends down its throat. When viewed in flight from below, it shows bold white wing linings, which are distinctive.

The Pileated Woodpecker is increasingly scarce throughout its range and is most often seen in Edmonton during the winter. Pairs continue to nest in the area, excavating large cavities in a decaying tree or stump. A pair will hollow out several nest holes in its territory and select one to shelter three or four white eggs. Both male and female build and tend the nest.

They feed on wood-boring insects and swiftly drill thumb-sized holes in pursuit of their prey.

The birds use their strong, bristled tail feathers to establish a three-point stance on the vertical side of a tree. This gives an extra drive to their highly efficient and noisy assault on the tree trunk. The call is a loud, high-pitched *kak-kak-kak*.

WESTERN WOOD-PEWEE

Contopus sordidulus
larger than sparrow-sized
Nests: June

THIS SWALLOW-SIZED woodland bird is more likely to be identified by its call than by its colours. It voices a distinct *pee-wee* or *pee-err* call which is unmistakable once identified.

The Western Wood-Pewee is a flycatcher and perches along streams, riverbanks, roadways and the edges of woods to attack flying insects. It nests more deeply in the woods of river valleys and forested areas, building a high cup-shaped nest of grass or bark-fibre bound with spider or insect webbing. It usually lays three eggs in its nest at the fork of a horizontal branch.

Present in Edmonton between May and September, the most frequent sightings in urban yards occur during spring and fall migrations. The call of the Western Wood-Pewee will be most often heard in the spring.

LEAST FLYCATCHER

Empidonax minimus
sparrow-sized
Nests: May - June

THIS TINY, restless bird, the size of a small sparrow, is welcomed in back yard gardens for its enthusiastic consumption of insects. Although comfortable in the lightly treed environment of an urban residential area during migration, it is a secretive bird, taking only short flights to capture small moths and flies and relying on the interior world of trees and large shrubs for much of its insect prey. It flits rapidly through branches only a few yards away from humans, although it will chase robins and jays should they intrude during the May to June nesting season.

The nest of the Least Flycatcher is a neat thin-walled cup in a central, well-disguised fork of a deciduous tree, often a larger fruit tree. In open parks of the city it will frequently nest in poplar and aspen. The four eggs are light buff or off-white. Its voice is surprising for its size, a strong *che-bek*.

The Least Flycatcher, present in Edmonton only in the summer months, winters as far south as Central America. Southward migration takes place in August, at which time large numbers of these birds pass through the Edmonton area.

EASTERN KINGBIRD

Tyrannus tyrannus
smaller than robin-sized
Nests: June

A CONSPICUOUS FLYCATCHER with sharply contrasting dull-black upperparts and white underparts, the Eastern Kingbird may be seen in Edmonton between May and September. A black tail, tipped with white, confirms the sighting. It is an unusually aggressive bird and attacks crows, magpies or hawks which presume on its nesting territory.

A pair of Eastern Kingbirds will select a site in a lightly-wooded area, choosing a stump, fence-post or a bare tree or shrub and nesting within a few feet of the ground, often next to water. Grasses, bark fibres and twine provide a deep nest for four white, mottled eggs.

Along with its typically fearless disposition, the Eastern Kingbird seems unafraid of humans and will readily nest in city parks or along open roadways. While hunting, it perches in a highly visible location, on a fence-post or open branch, and catches most of its prey on the wing with businesslike dispatch. Its call is a buzzing *dzeet*, although in attack or mating the cry becomes a loud and rising *kit-kit-kit*.

TREE SWALLOW
Tachycineta bicolor
sparrow-sized
Nests: June

A FEW TREE SWALLOWS are often back by late April: occasionally so early that some are caught by a late freeze. The bright, iridescent steely-blue back and white underparts distinguish this from other adult swallow species, and its graceful flights over ponds, marshes and fields are familiar sights, as the bird forages for insects.

Tree Swallows nest in tree cavities or old woodpecker holes, and make extensive use of bird boxes in open habitat such as on fences along fields. Flooded wooded areas, like those created by beaver dams, or areas with lots of standing dead timber, also offer choice nesting sites.

It is not unusual for nest boxes to be occupied by Tree Swallows even when they are placed fairly close to one another. A nest of grass lined with feathers is constructed inside the box or cavity. Four to six white eggs are laid, with incubation being undertaken by both sexes.

You can often see the male Tree Swallow perching for long periods on a fence or wire near the nest box. In late August, Tree Swallows will gather in large flocks before heading south to their winter territories.

The Barn Swallow, common in Edmonton from May to October, is easily identified by its elegant, long forked tail. The Barn Swallow makes its mud-plaster nest under the eaves of homes or garages on the outskirts of the city.

BLUE JAY
Cyanocitta cristata
robin-sized
Nests: May

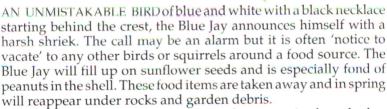

AN UNMISTAKABLE BIRD of blue and white with a black necklace starting behind the crest, the Blue Jay announces himself with a harsh shriek. The call may be an alarm but it is often 'notice to vacate' to any other birds or squirrels around a food source. The Blue Jay will fill up on sunflower seeds and is especially fond of peanuts in the shell. These food items are taken away and in spring will reappear under rocks and garden debris.

Jays are quite fearless and will attack cats, squirrels and other birds. Year-round residents, they eat whatever is in season — seeds, berries and insects — and sometimes will raid nests for eggs. They are usually found where there are conifers. During nesting season, the jay is quiet; the rest of the year it is a bird of many calls, from the harsh shriek to a gentle, watery trill.

Blue Jays have become quite numerous in Alberta in recent years. They are easy to attract to a feeding station and will set up a permanent residence in treed areas of the city. Inquisitive, quarrelsome and chatty, their presence is well worth the large quantities of seeds and peanuts they consume. When the feeder runs out, a scolding chatter will carry on until refills arrive.

BLACK-BILLED MAGPIE

Pica pica
larger than crow-sized
Nests: April

THIS MUST SURELY rank as one of the most easily recognized of urban birds. It has a deserved reputation as a scavenger and a pillager of small birds' nests, but despite this, it is a fascinating bird and it is interesting to contemplate how people would view it if it were not so common.

A year-round resident, the Black-billed Magpie is a handsome black and white bird with a long iridescent tail. It has not always been as common in Alberta as it is today. After largely disappearing with the loss of the bison, during the last century it has moved northwards with agricultural development and now it is found over most of the province. Nevertheless, it is a western bird and is not often found in the east.

Magpies make a fortress of a nest — a substantial stick structure with a roof and a grass-lined centre inside a strong clay basin — which they will build almost anywhere, even on the superstructure of a bridge.

AMERICAN CROW

Corvus brachyrhynchos
crow-sized
Nests: May

CROWS ARE a common sight in the city between April and October. They have adapted well to city life and can often be found taking advantage of human rubbish, whether hunting through garbage receptacles in the parks, foraging at the city dump, or keeping an ever watchful eye on household garbage bins. They are omnivorous birds: happy to eat grain and plant materials, they also take their toll of the eggs of ducks and upland game birds, and the nestlings of smaller birds. Much of their diet, however, is composed of insects.

American Crows nest in trees in the more wooded parts of the city. The nests are bulky assemblages of sticks, lined with soft grass and roots. Crows often refurbish old nests and those that have been used for a number of years can become quite large.

In fall, a flock will gather before migration. The big dark birds look particularly ominous in this mobbing period which in earlier times was called "a murder of crows." They will mob owls which are roosting in the open, which creates an easy way for birdwatchers to locate owls or hawks. The American Crow's call is a loud *caw*.

BLACK-CAPPED CHICKADEE

Parus atricapillus
smaller than sparrow-sized
Nests: May - June

ONE OF THE MOST commonly seen birds in the city, this year-round resident is found mainly in deciduous woods or in coniferous areas with a deciduous component. On a sunny winter's day after Christmas, it is not unusual to hear the males singing their *feebee* song. During the winter, chickadees spend their time feeding in flocks, which usually have distinct territories. In spring the birds disband into pairs and seek out suitable nest-holes, usually in a hole in a tree which they often enlarge. However, it is also possible to attract them to nest boxes in the backyard.

During the winter, chickadees are frequent visitors to the bird feeder, where they are fond of sunflower seeds and suet. They often take food off the feeder to eat in a nearby tree or to hide in bark crevices for retrieval at a later date. The Black-capped Chickadee is distinguishable from the less common Boreal Chickadee by its jet black, rather than brown, cap.

BOREAL CHICKADEE

Parus hudsonicus

sparrow-sized

Nests: In boreal forest

AS ITS NAME IMPLIES, this is not a bird of the prairies, but frequents coniferous woodland. It is not commonly seen in the city, but during the winter it sometimes joins Black-capped Chickadees as they forage through the trees. However, it may be a more frequent urban visitor than we suspect, as it is easily overlooked. But its voice is distinctive and is a useful clue to its presence: it sounds very much like a Black-capped Chickadee with a bad cold and laryngitis. From late March on, its *chee-wee-churn* song may be heard.

Boreal Chickadees are seen in Edmonton between September and April. Like Blackcapped Chickadees, Boreal Chickadees nest in holes in trees and they frequently excavate their own nest holes.

Boreal Chickadees frequent the coniferous ravines and bordering neighbourhoods. Look for them in the McKenzie, McKinnon, Patricia and Whitemud ravines.

RED-BREASTED NUTHATCH
Sitta canadensis

WHITE-BREASTED NUTHATCH
Sitta carolinensis
smaller than sparrow-sized
Nests: June

NUTHATCHES HAVE A VERY DISTINCTIVE shape and this together with their habit of feeding head down as they move from the top of the tree to the bottom, make them readily identifiable. They may have evolved this odd feeding strategy because it allows them to exploit the bark of trees for food that other birds have missed.

Both Red-Breasted Nuthatches and White-Breasted Nuthatches can be found in the city throughout the year, and they both come to feeders. The Red-Breasted Nuthatch is the more active and the more numerous of the two, although its numbers can vary greatly from one winter to the next. The Red-breasted Nuthatch is usually found associated with stands of coniferous trees. By contrast, the slightly larger White-Breasted Nuthatch is more common in deciduous trees.

Nuthatches nest in holes in trees, which they sometimes excavate themselves, although they also use natural cavities and old woodpecker holes. The Red-Breasted Nuthatch has an interesting habit of smearing resin around the entrance to its nest-hole: why, no one seems to know, but it may serve to reinforce the entrance hole and to stop larger birds from getting in.

Look for nuthatches in heavily wooded ravines and in the suburbs next to them.

Top: Red-breasted Nuthatch
Bottom: White-breasted Nuthatch

HOUSE WREN
Troglodytes aedon
smaller than sparrow-sized
Nests: May - June

ALTHOUGH THIS SMALL brown bird is not as commonly seen as the robin, it seems to have adapted just about as well to city dwelling. A back yard with some thick shrubbery, or any thick vegetation, will often contain a pair of these small birds. To attract them to the back yard, put up a nest box amid the Virginia creeper or in a quiet shrubby corner, protected from the household cat.

House Wrens spend much of the day scolding everything in sight, and have a wonderful song which they sing particularly in the early mornings. The birds feed mainly on small insects and so, not surprisingly, they are summer visitors, arriving somewhat later than most migrants in May and departing in September.

They have more than one brood each year and frequently change mates between broods.

RUBY-CROWNED KINGLET

Regulus calendula
smaller than sparrow-sized
Nests: June

THIS SMALL BIRD favours large coniferous trees and mixed wood forests. It will come into shrubbery in the yard when on migration, when it can be found looking for insects in the branches.

Ruby-crowned Kinglets arrive in Edmonton in May. They make a wonderful nest under the end of a branch of a coniferous tree, from lichens, mosses and spiderwebs.

The Ruby-Crowned Kinglet has a surprisingly loud song for such a small bird and its whistled phrases are one of the best clues to its presence early in the spring. It is a small, dark green bird, always on the move and constantly flicking its wings as it flits from branch to branch while feeding.

By September most birds are on the move south again, as at about then the supply of insects on which Ruby-Crowned Kinglets survive is starting to dwindle.

The Golden-Crowned Kinglet, which is identified by its black-rimmed yellow crown and white eye-stripe, is also a resident of Edmonton, and is eagerly sought by birdwatchers.

MOUNTAIN BLUEBIRD

Sialia currucoides
smaller than robin-sized
Nests: May - June

THE MOUNTAIN BLUEBIRD is misnamed, as it is found throughout most of the province, with the exception of the extreme north. Although it is not an urban bird, it is frequently found around buildings in rural areas and on the outskirts of the city. It is easily attracted to nesting boxes in these situations and many people have put nesting boxes for Mountain Bluebirds on fence-posts beside the highway. Bluebirds need this type of habitat as their feeding pattern requires a low perch from which they can spot insects on or just above the ground.

The birds are fairly comfortable near humans, and it is intriguing to watch them searching for and catching insects. A few years ago, their numbers had declined quite considerably, perhaps due to competition for nest sites from European Starlings and House Sparrows, two very aggressive birds that arrived here comparatively recently. However, thanks to the introduction of bluebird nesting boxes, the numbers of Mountain Bluebirds are once again increasing.

SWAINSON'S THRUSH

Catharus ustulatus
smaller than robin-sized
Nests: June

FORMERLY KNOWN AS the Olive-backed Thrush, the Swainson's Thrush can be distinguished from other thrush species by its buff-brown eye-rings and cheeks. This summer resident of Edmonton is elusive, spending much of its time searching for insects deep and low in wooded areas. It is most easily identified by its appealing song, spiralling upward from phrase to phrase: listen for it particularly at sunset and at dawn.

The Swainson's Thrush winters in Mexico and South America, and breeds throughout much of Canada. Its two to five blue eggs, evenly marked with light brown, are incubated by the female for about 12 days. The bird usually builds its nest of twigs, grasses and moss in low evergreen trees or bushes in areas with a coniferous-deciduous mixture, although it will occasionally nest in deciduous trees or shrubs.

Favouring alder and willow stands, Swainson's Thrushes are also found in recently burned areas which are experiencing new growth.

The Hermit Thrush, also seen in Edmonton in summer, is a sparrow-sized bird with the same configurations as its near relative the robin. It is olive-brown above with a rufous tail and whitish below. Its habit of flicking its wings and tail is a more certain identifier. The song of the Hermit Thrush is broken into phrases as it spirals upward, each phrase starting higher than the one which went before. There is a pause between each set of phrases.

AMERICAN ROBIN

Turdus migratorius
robin-sized
Nests: May - July

THE ROBIN, perhaps more than any other, is a prime example of how well some birds can adapt to the human environment. It seems as much at home in our back yards and alleys as it does in its more natural setting of forest clearings and riverbanks. It is also an urban harbinger of spring, and the first robin in March is the most traditional sign that the seasons are changing.

The males sing from house tops, trees and telephone wires to define their territories and two males may be seen fighting on the ground in a territorial dispute. The birds nest in trees and in suitable recesses in buildings, where they build a sturdy nest of stems and grass. The nest is lined with mud and fine grass. The eggs are a pale blue colour and it is not unusual to find an eggshell on the ground. If it is chipped neatly in half around the middle, the chances are that the egg has just hatched and the parent has disposed of the shell.

BOHEMIAN WAXWING

Bombycilla garrulus
larger than sparrow-sized
Nests: Northern forest

THESE WINTER VISITORS are a familiar sight in this city; in fact, Edmonton holds the world's record for Bohemian Waxwing occurance. For most of the winter they feed in flocks on berries — particularly those of the mountain ash — their wheezy, chattering call readily giving them away. As the winter draws to an end the flocks often become very large, and prior to the birds' migrating north to breed it is not uncommon to see hundreds of waxwings together.

In years when the berry crop is poor, the birds do not stay in the city, but fly to other wintering grounds where there is sufficient food.

When you see a flock of waxwings, look for a predator, the Merlin. This small falcon is relatively common in the city and is frequently seen chasing waxwings. In those years when waxwings are not common, Merlins tend also to be scarce.

Bohemian Waxwings show white patches on the wings and chestnut brown undertail coverts, which distinguish them from Cedar Waxwings.

CEDAR WAXWING

Bombycilla cedrorum
larger than sparrow-sized
Nests: June

THIS HANDSOME BIRD has an overall sleek appearance, with a very smooth-looking plumage. The breast has a yellowish wash. Red wax-like extensions of the secondary wing feathers give the bird its name. Unlike the Bohemian Waxwing which is a winter vistor to Edmonton, the smaller Cedar Waxwing is seen primarily in summer.

Cedar Waxwings can be found along the edges of most wooded habitats, whether open forest, city parks or the back yard. They are common in our river valleys. Except during the breeding season when they pair off, waxwings spend most of their time in flocks. This is a good strategy against predators, such as Merlins: flocking often confuses a predator and gives the individual a better chance to get away. In addition, many pairs of eyes are better than a single pair for detecting predators.

This bird nests out on the branch of a tree or bush. The nest is constructed from a wide variety of materials, depending on what is available — an assortment of plant matter including lichens and roots may be used, along with paper, dog hair, twine and whatever else can be found. The blue-grey eggs are spotted with black or brown.

NORTHERN SHRIKE

Lanius excubitor
robin-sized
Nests: Nests in far north

THEIR "ROBBER" FACE MASKS give Northern Shrikes the looks of brigands. These robin-sized birds, and the similar but slightly smaller Loggerhead Shrikes which are occasionally seen in Edmonton in summer, are sometimes called "butcher birds" because of their technique of hanging small prey on barbed wire, thorns, or in the forks of branches.

Although shrikes have the beaks of carnivorous birds, they do not have the talons. They prefer high perches and have a distinctive flight pattern, dropping suddenly from their perches with rapid wing strokes, and flying near the ground before abruptly rising again at the next perch.

Primarily seen in Edmonton during migration in April in October, the Northern Shrike occasionally overwinters here. It is one of the few birds which sing during the winter season — a mixture of melodious whistles interrupted by harsher sounds. It nests in the sub-arctic.

Left: Northern Shrike
Inset: Loggerhead Shrike

EUROPEAN STARLING

Sturnus vulgaris
smaller than robin-sized
Nests: May - June

THIS BLACK BIRD is a familiar sight in the city, a truly urban bird that is here year round. The first starlings were brought to New York from Europe in 1890; they have since spread rapidly and are now common over most of this continent. In fact, they are so widespread that they have become a major threat to native nesting species, such as Tree Swallows, Mountain Bluebirds and Downy Woodpeckers. They were first seen in Edmonton in 1948.

Starlings are really woodland-edge birds, but they are remarkably adaptable and their principal needs are a supply of suitable nesting holes and plenty of nearby grassy areas over which to feed. They nest in old woodpecker holes or in a broken tree branch, but they are just as much at home under the eaves of a house. They find the well-cut grass of back yards and city parks very much to their liking and they do an immense amount of good feeding on insect grubs. They will also occasionally visit bird feeders.

Starlings are wonderful mimics and incorporate snatches of other birds' songs into their own. They also imitate many city noises, including the squeak of garage doors and dog whistles. Although many European Starlings fly south in the winter, some can be seen on the coldest days, huddled over a chimney to keep warm. In winter, their breasts and bellies are speckled with whitish spots, and their beaks are black.

RED-EYED VIREO

Vireo olivaceus
sparrow-sized
Nests: June

THE RED-EYED VIREO is the only vireo with a red eye which, unfortunately, can be very hard to see. The crown of its head is greyish, but over the eye there is a broad whitish stripe which is bordered on each side by a black line. The bird lacks wing bars.

Although dull-coloured and hard to distinguish in the field, it is a characteristic species of the aspen woodland. The bird is a persistent singer, its song delivered tirelessly throughout the day, even on the hottest afternoons when other birds are silent.

The Red-eyed Vireo inhabits primarily broad-leaved trees and tall shrubbery. Here, in a slow deliberate pattern, it forages among the leaves for insects. It may be difficult to see among the leaves, but once you are familiar with its song you will detect its distinctive darting flight.

Usually the nest is constructed about two to four metres from the ground. It is a well-made cup suspended by its edge in the fork of a branch. Look for the empty nests in winter when they are not obscured by foliage.

Although sightings are uncommon, the Solitary Vireo is frequently heard in summer in coniferous areas of parks, and the river valley underbrush. Its song, very like that of the Red-eyed Vireo, is loud and melodious but slurred. To some the notes paraphrase the word *vireo* which announces in Latin, "I am green."

YELLOW WARBLER

Dendroica petechia
smaller than sparrow-sized
Nests: May - June

THIS BRIGHT YELLOW warbler may be mistaken for an escaped canary. It is the most common and most widely distributed of all the wood warblers in the province, and is as likely to be seen in the city as in the more remote parts of the province. The males start singing in early May, as soon as they arrive, to establish their territories. It is then, before the trees leaf out, that these bright yellow birds are most likely to be seen. Later in the season, despite their bright colour, they are much harder to spot as they search for insects in the tree canopies. The male's call is a very simple one to remember — *sweet-sweet-sweet-so-sweet* — which he usually gives while sitting at the top of a small tree.

The Yellow Warbler builds a nest made of grasses and lined with plant down, and its four or five eggs are white with brown speckles. Most warblers have left the province by the middle of September.

Look also for the Tennessee Warbler, commonly seen and heard in Edmonton, which has olive-greenish wings, a white chest and dark eye-stripes. Although the female's underparts may be tinged with yellow, the Tennessee Warbler is more often mistaken for a vireo than for another warbler.

YELLOW-RUMPED WARBLER

Dendroica coronata
smaller than sparrow-sized
Nests: June

THE RACE OF this species that is most frequently seen in the city was at one time called the Myrtle Warbler, and those nearer the mountains were called Audubon's Warblers. They have been found to interbreed and are therefore now considered a single species. The more eastern race is depicted here, but watch for the yellow-throated Audubon's race, particularly during spring migration.

The Yellow-rumped Warbler is likely to nest in a conifer, building a small cup of twigs and grass lined with feathers, and laying four or five white eggs with grey and brown specks.

Though tiny, the Yellow-rumped Warbler is a conspicuous bird as it flits about after insects. Its song is a weak *seet-seet-seet-seet-trrr*. It prefers the edge of coniferous clumps while pursuing its prey but is often found near water in the evening. Although not commonly seen during summer, the Yellow-rumped Warbler is abundant during migration.

AMERICAN REDSTART
Setophaga ruticilla
smaller than sparrow-sized
Nests: June - July

ITS SHOWY COLOURS and constant activity, along with its *zee-zee-zee-zwee* song, make this flashy warbler immediately recognizable.

The redstart migrates to Alberta nesting grounds in May. It nests only where there is significant wooded area, but relies on small open spaces when hunting insects. The nest is well built and settled in an upright crotch of a poplar or large shrub. The cup-shaped nest will likely contain four light-grey, spotted eggs.

A summer visitor, the American Redstart is most likely to be seen in back yards during migration. It is unceasingly active, but its startling orange, black and white colouration make it unmistakable. A black head will indicate a male of at least two years. Females and young have yellow on both the wing and tail. Orange display patches on the male are on the sides, wings and at the lower rump or base of the tail.

WESTERN TANAGER
Piranga ludoviciana
larger than sparrow-sized
Nests: June

THE BRILLIANT RED HEAD and canary-yellow body of the male Western Tanager are likely to be seen in the city only during late spring. In its late summer migration south, the head will have lost much of the red in its feathers. The female is yellow-green above and yellow below.

Berries in the yard are a principal attraction for Western Tanagers in August. They are calm birds and prefer to remain in the interior canopy of trees or large shrubs, such as mature lilacs. In the spring tanagers feed on insects, often plucking them out of the air in the manner of flycatchers.

The tanager nest is a frail, shallow saucer woven of rootlets, grass and weeds in the horizontal fork of a coniferous or dense poplar tree. Three to five bluish-green speckled eggs will yield chicks which mature rapidly.

CHIPPING SPARROW

Spizella passerina
smaller than sparrow-sized
Nests: June

ONE OF THE smallest sparrows that visits the city, the Chipping Sparrow has a red-brown cap bordered by white eyebrow stripes.

The Chipping Sparrow spends much of its time feeding inconspicuously on the ground, but after the hatch, it concentrates on insects.

Chipping Sparrows will nest readily in a well treed urban environment, preferring conifers but content with dense shrubs or hedges. The nest is a neat cup of grasses, weeds and, quite often, animal hair. The average of four eggs are pale blue with brown, black and purple markings on the larger end.

The male will usually be well hidden while singing its insect-like trill. The call is a high sweet *seep* or *siip*. The Chipping Sparrow is a May to September visitor to Edmonton.

WHITE-THROATED SPARROW

Zonotrichia albicollis
sparrow-sized
Nests: June

ITS SONG IS LIKELY to be heard before the bird is sighted, beginning with two clear whistles follow by a series of three-noted whistles. This is often patriotically paraphrased as *Dear-Old-Canada-Canada-Canada*.

It makes its home on the ground or underbrush, and can be seen throughout the summer in the river valley or in wooded parkland with suitable low cover. It is also occasionally found in open parkland. The cup nest of mosses, coarse grasses and rootlets is lined with fine grasses or hair, and contains three to five greenish-white eggs with spotted marking on the blunter end.

A summer resident of Edmonton between April and September, it is most likely to be seen at the feeder in May or September. Its yellow lores (the space between the bill and the eye) and dark bill distinguish it from the similar White-crowned Sparrow, which can also have a white throat.

WHITE-CROWNED SPARROW

Zonotrichia leucophrys

sparrow-sized

Nests: June

PATCHES OF OPEN GROUND or grass with low brushes nearby are the critical elements in the habitat of this long-tailed sparrow. Although not a characteristic summer species in Edmonton, it frequently shows up on city lawns on migration, usually in early May or mid-September and often in a flock of twenty or thirty birds. Fallen seeds make up much of its diet.

The song of the White-crowned Sparrow is a clear whistle followed by a series of three quivering notes of a different pitch. This song is most likely to be heard in the foothills, during nesting season.

DARK-EYED JUNCO

Junco hyemalis
sparrow-sized
Nests: May

THE BIRD ILLUSTRATED here, formerly known as a Slate-coloured Junco, is one of two races of juncos in Alberta which are now identified together as Dark-eyed Juncos. The Slate-coloured race is more commonly seen in Edmonton. The adult male of the Oregon race has a dark grey hood which covers its head, while its back and wings are brown. In both races, the pinkish bill is a distinctive colouration.

The Dark-eyed Junco is a friendly bird and a frequent companion on spring walks in the river valley. The males return first from the annual migration to the U.S. and compete with other sparrows at the bird feeder. Females, which may arrive two weeks later, have a brownish tint, similar to the fledglings. The birds spend a good deal of time on the ground, near shrubs and trees, looking for seeds and dried berries. The domestic cat seems to be their principal urban predator. A group of juncos will be alerted by the flash of white outer tail feathers as the first of them takes flight, voicing a sharp, dry *chit-atit* of warning.

The junco will likely breed in coniferous woods, in a small grass and moss nest set on the ground beneath a brush-pile or tangled shrub. Three to five pale green eggs are speckled with brown.

SNOW BUNTING

Plectrophenax nivalis
sparrow-sized
Nests: In high arctic

THIS IS A BIRD of the Arctic, where it breeds on the coast and islands. It visits Alberta in winter, often arriving just before the first snows. The Snow Bunting prefers the open country: look for it in fields on the outskirts of Edmonton, where huge flocks may be seen feeding together. They remain inconspicuous while on the ground — perfectly camouflaged by their brown and white plumage — but every few minutes the flock will take off briefly and become quite obvious. Snow Buntings rarely perch in bushes or trees, as they usually roost on the ground. They are often found on quiet rural roads, and vehicle headlights may illuminate hundreds of small white birds which have been startled up into the air.

Snow Buntings leave for their northern breeding grounds in April; during this time those that have wintered to the south move through central Alberta in huge flocks.

RED-WINGED BLACKBIRD

Agelaius phoeniceus
smaller than robin-sized
Nests: May - June

THE CALL of the Red-winged Blackbird in the spring announces a change in the season. In and around Edmonton from April to October, the adult males are hard to miss with their bright red wing patches, which they use to warn off males from adjoining territories. The size of the wing patch and the way the bird uses it during its display is directly related to how successful the male is in attracting a mate or group of females which will nest in his territory. The female, by contrast, is far less conspicuous and can appear to be a totally different species. She is a heavily striped bird with a marked buffy streak over the eye.

Look for Red-winged Blackbirds in wet areas beside ponds, lakes and alongside the river where they often nest in loose colonies. The colonies are often very noisy with the distinctive *o-k-a-ree-a* call of the males and frequent territorial disputes. The rough-grass nests are often built on two or more cattail stalks over water.

WESTERN MEADOWLARK

Sturnella neglecta
robin-sized
Nests: May - July

THE WESTERN MEADOWLARK is one of the earliest of the migrant birds to arrive in the province, arriving here in March and staying until October. It is fond of perching on the highest object available, often a fence post, from where it sings one of the most melodic songs of any bird found in Alberta: *pee-wee pee-weeoo*. It is very much a bird of the open county and to find it, look around the edges of the city. The Western Meadowlark is difficult to miss with its bright yellow breast with a black V across the front.

It builds its nest on the ground, cleverly disguised in a clump, with an entrance at the side. Its eggs are white, speckled and blotched with brown and purple.

Western Meadowlarks have apparently spread north in the province with the development of farming. Formerly they were restricted to the south but now nest as far north as the Peace River country. They seem to do well on farmland as long as there is enough rough grass between fields
or at the sides of the road.

YELLOW-HEADED BLACKBIRD

Xanthocephalus xanthocephalus
robin-sized
Nests: May - June

THE YELLOW-HEADED BLACKBIRD is much more particular about the habitat it prefers than is the Red-winged Blackbird. Both like wet areas, but where the Red-winged Blackbird seems relatively at home near any damp area — even a ditch — the Yellow-headed Blackbird prefers to nest alongside deeper, larger bodies of water. The males spend a great deal of their time singing and chasing other intruding males out of their territories: the song is a rasping note, like the sound of a rusty hinge. The nest of the Yellow-headed Blackbird is nearly always built over water, in cattails and reeds.

The males display using white wing patches, and frequently perch on the tallest objects in their territories. The females are brown and mottled and spend most of their nesting time incubating the eggs.

Yellow-headed Blackbirds are seen in the Edmonton area from April to September.

NORTHERN ORIOLE
Icterus galbula
smaller than robin-sized
Nests: June

THE NORTHERN ORIOLE is one of the most striking birds to be seen in Edmonton, with its vivid golden-orange underparts and rump and black back and head, yet it is not an obvious bird. It spends most of its time high up in tall deciduous trees, often in parks along the river valley, where it feeds and nests. Its clear distinct whistle, *chuck-chuck-wheu-wheu-wheu-wheu*, or *peter-peter-peter* may help in locating it. The female is less vividly coloured, being olive above and dull yellow-orange below.

Orioles arrive in the city in May when the trees are in leaf, and build nests which look like hanging baskets out of grass, shredded bark and other plant material. These are suspended from the branches by fibres such as bark, string or hair. Four to six eggs are laid and hatch in a mere 12 to 15 days. Early in the season orioles feed on insects and will even consume hairy larvae which are often shunned by other birds: they are one of the few birds to eat the tent caterpillars which infest our aspen trees. Later in the season fruits of saskatoon, cherry and other shrubs are eaten before the long migration in September.

PINE GROSBEAK
Pinicola enucleator
smaller than robin-sized
Nests: June

THE ROSE-RED HEAD, breast and back of the male Pine Grosbeak is quite often seen within the city during harsh winters. The male is the showier bird while the female, at a distance, looks olive-grey except for the white wing bars. The tail is noticeably longer than is that of the Evening Grosbeak. The two species sometimes feed together — on leftover seeds and the fruit and berries of ornamental trees, particularly northern mountain maple. Even in the winter, however, Pine Grosbeaks will spend much of their time eating the seeds of conifers. They can be found pursuing the same wild diet during summer in the mountain parks, where the young hatch in late June from light green eggs speckled with brown.

Within the city, the adults and immature birds are relatively tame. The male plumage may be confused with that of the Purple Finch, a smaller bird that is not known to winter here. The White-winged Crossbill also has a similar appearance. The Rose-breasted Grosbeak is a summer visitor to Edmonton, nesting in our river valley.

PURPLE FINCH

Carpodacus purpureus
smaller than sparrow-sized
Nests: Late May - June

THE FIRST GLIMPSE of it at a bird feeder can be startling. The impression is of a wine-coloured bird with the head more red than purple. It is sparrow-sized but the beak is quite thick and does not cross at the tip which would, instead, identify a Red or White-winged Crossbill. The brown-grey female and immature male are also identifiable by the heavy short beak which can crush the harder seeds in a feeder.

Nests for the Purple Finch within an urban area are likely to be on a horizontal branch of a spruce, although all large shade trees are possible sites. The nest is built of twigs, coarse grass and rootlets, lined with fine grass. The shallow cup may hold from four to six eggs.

An early spring can encourage the first Purple Finches to arrive in late April and they may remain until early October.

The song of the male Purple Finch is a long, musical warble; in flight, a sharp, metallic *pik*. Gardeners note that the Purple Finch will sometimes eat the centres of newly opened flowers.

RED CROSSBILL

Loxia curvirostra
sparrow-sized
Nests: anytime

AS THE NAME SUGGESTS, crossbills have a unique beak, with the large upper mandible crossing over the lower mandible. This looks awkward until you see the birds using their beaks to extract the seeds of conifer cones; the perfection of the shape then becomes obvious. The Red Crossbill is a medium-sized finch (16 cm in length). The males have a red head and breast and a red-brown back. The females are yellow and brown and the young are mottled on the breast and head, with a brown back and wings.

This species is highly irregular in its distribution. In some years it is very common in coniferous woodland, but in a poor year for coniferous seed cone production, the birds move elsewhere. The crossbill is unusual in that it breeds at almost any time of the year. The birds move about in loose flocks and the *jip-jip* calls and the remains of cones on the ground are good indications of their presence.

Watch also for the White-winged Crossbill, which looks similar but has two very obvious white wing bars. While Red Crossbills are associated with pine trees; White-winged Crossbills favour spruce.

COMMON REDPOLL

Carduelis flammea
smaller than sparrow-sized
Nests: in Arctic

COMMON REDPOLLS HAVE the pert plumpness of a chickadee and are about the same size, but are exclusively winter birds. Both the Common Redpoll and the less frequently seen Hoary Redpoll arrive with heavy frost and are unlikely to remain beyond April.

The two species intermingle readily and both are sometimes found at the bird feeder. Both have red caps and black chins but the Hoary Redpoll has a frosty colouration and white rump. The two species can be quite difficult to distinguish from one another.

These cheery finches are found in weedy ditches, shrubbery and seed trees, particularly birches. A sheltered bird feeder is likely to bring repeated visits if established in the early part of the winter.

Both species have a twittering song and call with a rattling *chit-chit-chit-chit*.

PINE SISKIN

Carduelis pinus
smaller than sparrow-sized
Nests: May - June

THESE ACROBATIC BIRDS can be a delight around a feeder. Like chickadees they hang upside down or sideways when feeding, usually hunting for the seeds in pine cones but also pecking at crevices in deciduous or conifer bark for insects. Their enthusiasm for dandelion seeds is also cheering.

In flocks, Pine Siskins are calmer birds than their near cousins, the redpolls and the goldfinches. The yellow in their wing primaries and tails is not very noticeable when they are perching, but is immediately visible in flight.

The nest, a cup of fine twigs and rootlets, is usually located in a conifer. Four to six pale blue, lightly spotted eggs are laid.

Siskins rarely sing except in flight, a scratchy *shik-shik* and sometime a light *sheee*. Although Pine Siskins occasionally over-winter in Edmonton, they are most commonly seen here between March and October.

AMERICAN GOLDFINCH

Carduelis tristis
smaller than sparrow-sized
Nests: July

A STUBBY BILL and stubby tail distinguish this small yellow bird from the Yellow Warbler, which has no black in its plumage. The only other bright yellow bird in Alberta with black cap and wings is the much larger Evening Grosbeak. The female lacks the distinctive colouration of the male and, aside from the sparrow-like (seed-eating) beak, looks like a small warbler or vireo.

The American Goldfinch can be seen throughout the summer in both back yard and park. It is not shy and will readily move near to humans while it hunts seeds on the ground or flits through the branches of trees and tall shrubs. It is particularly fond of feeding on thistle seeds. Its nest of grass among low branches can contain from three to seven pale blue eggs.

The roller-coaster flight of the American Goldfinch is unmistakable: a long swoop and abrupt lift followed by quick wing strokes. The same pattern is repeated. Its song sounds like *potato chips* to some ears but is more accurately rendered as a four syllable *per-chic-o-ree.*

EVENING GROSBEAK

Coccothraustes vespertinus
larger than sparrow-sized
Nests: June - July

THE EVENING GROSBEAK is most commonly seen in winter, feeding in flocks on maple seeds, small crabapples or mountain ash berries. However it isn't very far away in spring and summer. The Evening Grosbeak doesn't migrate — it just disappears into conifers or mixed wood stands where it nests very high up and is difficult to find.

When food becomes scarce, Evening Gros-beaks flock and enter more populated areas. They feed on available berries, but can be tempted to try sunflowers seeds at a feeding station. They've been nicknamed "evening greedies" because it doesn't take much to tempt them.

The plumage is elegant: black, white and yellow. Females and young have a hint of silvery-grey. The Evening Grosbeak is a plump bird with a distinctive, undulating flight pat-tern. The large white wing patches are very noticeable in flight.

Its most frequent call is a clear *cleep-cleep*.

HOUSE (ENGLISH) SPARROW

Passer domesticus
smaller than sparrow-sized
Nests: June - July

THE HOUSE SPARROW is a stocky, noisy little bird with black throat and bib and chestnut markings. The female is dull gray and unmarked, often confused with other sparrows.

Sparrows are often seen in flocks. They inhabit both urban and rural settings, surviving well wherever there is human settlement. The species is not native to this continent, but was introduced in the 1850s. It is extremely adaptable.

Sparrows will nest anywhere, even occasionally in the branches of trees. They are especially fond of bird houses or boxes set out to attract native species, and are very hard to discourage. There is usually more than one hatch of 3 to 7 eggs each year.

House Sparrows are voracious eaters, and they will respond quickly to bread crumbs or picnic leftovers in summer. Feeders intended for small birds can be protected from sparrows by a wire mesh.

While generally a pesky nuisance, their loud chirps outside the window on a cold winter day can warm the heart and serve as a reminder that the bitter cold is not lifeless.

ATTRACTING BIRDS

GETTING STARTED at birdwatching need not cost a lot of money. Many people derive a great deal of pleasure by simply putting out household scraps for birds on a homemade feeder, close enough to the window that birds can be seen as they come and go.

It is certainly not necessary to be able to identify all the birds at the feeder to be able to enjoy them, but there is a great sense of satisfaction in being able to tell one species from another. Human nature being what it is, we tend to want to learn.

Most people interested in watching birds use binoculars, as this allows them to identify key characteristics such as plumage, leg colour, and bill shape. Binoculars also allow the user to watch the more timid birds that normally stay at a distance or remain in the cover of bushes and trees, and they allow us to study birds' behaviour. Small details help to build the overall picture of a bird, which helps to identify the species.

Buying binoculars is perhaps the biggest financial outlay the birdwatcher will make, but it is not necessary to spend a great deal of money as there are many inexpensive but good models. Buying

An attractive back yard offers many birdwatching opportunities.

binoculars can be confusing, and much has been written about how to choose a pair. The best advice is to ask another bird-watcher. Remember that no one pair will be perfect for every situation — watching birds in woodland requires binoculars with a wide field of view but a reasonably low magnification (7 - 8X would be ideal), whereas watching shorebirds by a river bank would require a higher magnification, and a telescope would then be useful. Binoculars tend to get heavy around the neck, and it is a good idea to keep this in mind when selecting the right pair. A wider neck strap certainly helps, but if you have a choice, you will not regret going for the lightest pair that seems to be right for you. Durability and brightness will also be factors in the binoculars you choose.

Belted Kingfisher in the river valley.

If you like watching waterfowl and shorebirds at the local slough, you may be tempted by the higher magnification of a spotting telescope, mounted on a tripod for stability.

Aside from binoculars, however, the only other piece of equipment you really need is a field guide that will enable you to identify the birds you see. Armed with a pair of binoculars and a good field guide, you will find a whole new world opening up for you as you take advantage of the many excellent birdwatching sites in and around the city, or enjoy your own back yard birds more.

Soon, you will be taking your binoculars with you on a hike or as you take the dog for a walk in the park — the opportunities for their use are endless.

BIRD FEEDERS

Why bother with a bird feeder in your back yard? The great advantage is that by feeding birds on a regular basis, they learn to come to that spot every day and as more birds learn, the numbers of species and individuals increase. Your back yard can become your own bird sanctuary.

Feeders may also provide advantages for birds. They are used much more frequently when natural food sources are less abundant — particularly in the winter months. Here in Alberta, the winters can be long and hard, and the birds using neighbourhood feeders may need to rely on this food source for survival. Once feeding is started, it should be maintained throughout the winter and particularly during the most severe weather. A break in the

Blue Jays feeding at a tray feeder.

Black-capped Chickadees at a seed dispenser.

normal routine may mean that the birds you have so carefully attracted will move on or, if the weather is unusually bitter, not survive. Try feeding the birds at the same time each day and you will notice how they quickly adjust to a daily routine. Early morning is best. Better still, provide sufficient food to last two or three days.

There may only be a few birds at the feeder at any one time, but this does not necessarily mean that only a few birds are using the feeder. It can be difficult to recognize individuals, but by banding and watching them as they come back to feeders, it has been shown that birds use feeders for only short periods during the day. Any one feeder may be visited by many individuals throughout the daylight hours as they forage through the neighbourhood. This is normal, particularly in the winter when they must range over a much wider area to find the variety of foods they need to sustain themselves.

When you place a feeder in the garden, don't expect the birds to find it immediately. It often takes a few weeks for numbers to build up, so persevere and be patient.

It is best to position the feeder some distance from the house, as the birds will be wary if they see movement. Find a site that is likely to be attractive to birds: immediately adjacent to trees or bushes for instance, rather than in the centre of the lawn. Immediate escape cover is as important as the food itself. Small birds are innately aware of the danger of avian predators such as Merlins, and will soon take a liking to a feeder that offers safety as well as good fare.

Bear in mind also that cats can be a real threat, so make it difficult for them by ensuring that the birds have a chance to see them. Avoid positioning your feeder right beside a suitable hiding place, such as a low bush, and make sure that it is high enough to be out of reach of the agile cat — which can leap as high as two metres. A large circle of page wire under the feeder will soon dissuade the neighbour's Tabby.

There are countless designs for bird feeders, but essentially they all do exactly the same job: they dispense food that birds will eat in a convenient and hygienic manner. Depending on the type of birds one wishes to attract, there are four basic designs:

- hanging seed dispensers for bird-seed
- tray feeders for mixed bird foods
- suet feeders
- hummingbird feeders

Hanging Seed Dispensers

These come in many different designs, but if you bear a few points in mind it is easy to select the right one.

The feeder should be large enough to hold a good supply of seeds; otherwise, you will be forever refilling it. The ease with

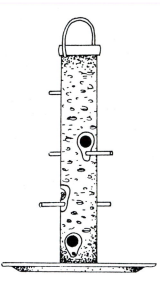

A simple seed dispenser, well designed with perches for birds and a feeding tray at the bottom. Very attractive to Black-capped Chickadees.

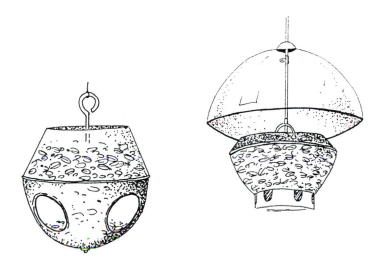

LEFT: A larger seed dispenser that holds more food has larger openings to allow bigger birds to use it.
RIGHT: A seed hopper with a plastic dome that keeps off squirrels and larger birds. It has good seed capacity and is for smaller birds.

which the feeder can be filled is also important. Birds will eat most during the coldest periods, so you'll need a feeder that is easy to open and close on a cold day with your gloves on.

All feeders should be cleaned regularly, so they should be easy to take apart. The seed should be protected from the rain and snow. Although they tend to break easily and must then be replaced, clear plastic seed containers are the best — they clean easily, are reasonably strong, allow you to see when they need refilling, and allow the birds to see what is inside them.

Squirrels will gnaw on feeders to enlarge their openings, so feeders with metal openings may prove useful.

There are many commercial seed mixtures available for hanging feeders, but a surprising number of birds seem to prefer sunflower seeds: if you put up two feeders, one with a mixture and one with sunflower seeds, you will be able to observe the preferences yourself.

Tray Feeders

This type of feeder can be designed to attract many different types of birds, from seed eaters to those that forage on the ground. Some tray feeders have a hopper, with the tray immediately below to catch the seed and provide a feeding area. These work well, but have some disadvantages. There is never enough room for all the birds to feed without overcrowding, and so the more dominant species and individuals tend to drive others away. It is also quite difficult to see the birds at the feeder. The more timid ones tend to feed on the side furthest from your sight — a problem which can be overcome if you arrange to have only one outlet.

Perhaps the best type of tray feeder is one which is nothing more than a large tray, onto which seed and other scraps are spread. It should have a lip to stop too much food from spilling or blowing onto the ground. But don't worry about the spillage; you will find that many species prefer to feed on the ground under the feeder. Position this type of feeder near some tree or shrub cover. And again, a temporary wire fence with at least 10 cm mesh will keep the cat from lunging directly under the feeder, yet will allow casual access for even the larger birds.

A tray-type feeder with a hopper that has see-through side for easy checking of food levels.

Suet Feeders

You can get beef suet from the meat counter at the supermarket and birds such as woodpeckers and chickadees love it. It is a good high-energy food for birds in cold weather and is easy to feed as it comes in a lump, lasts a while, and can be simply suspended in an old onion bag or from a string. Other types of suet feeders can be made using wire mesh: the plastic-coated type is best, as birds can damage themselves on normal metal mesh especially in cold weather. If you have the tools, bore holes in a short log and push suet into the holes, then hang this up.

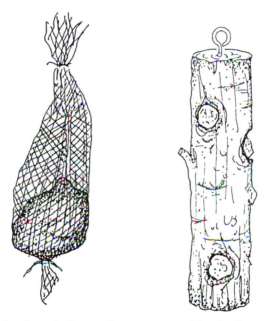

LEFT: The simplest of all suet dispensers: an old onion bag, easily replaceable.
RIGHT: A more natural type of suet dispenser. An old log with holes drilled in it and stuffed with suet.

Hummingbird Feeders

It is possible to attract hummingbirds into your garden with a colourful variety of flowers, but a good hummingbird feeder is one of the best ways to keep them coming back. When buying a feeder, look closely at the seals that keep the fluid in the container and choose one that looks well made. Most of them work, but the cheaper ones don't last long and frequently drip. This attracts wasps, bees and ants and leaves the feeder empty in short order. A hummingbird feeder should have some red on it, as this helps to attract the birds. You can make your own feeding fluid by dissolving one part white sugar in three to four parts near-boiling water, then letting it cool. Experiment and see what concentration seems to be preferred. There is no need to add red dye to the liquid, and never use honey as this ferments readily and may grow a mold that can be fatal to hummingbirds. It is important to clean the feeder frequently. In warm weather, add only a bit of liquid each time and let your feathered visitors consume it before it ferments. Keep the refill jar in the refrigerator.

Because hummingbirds are so small, it is most rewarding to hang the feeder near a window, or on the deck, where the birds quickly become accustomed to people and will allow you to watch at close range.

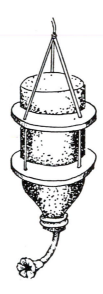

A home-made hummingbird feeder. Use an artificial red flower at the mouth.

Nest Boxes

Different species of birds have evolved to take advantage of different habitats. Each species uses a different feeding strategy and a different nesting strategy. By providing a variety of different types of food at your feeder, it is possible to attract ground-feeding birds and tree-feeding birds, seed eaters, omnivorous birds and even the odd bird of prey. The same is true if one provides a variety of different nesting opportunities. Birds will be attracted to artificial sites during the breeding season. Although some boxes may not be used the first year, they can be relocated next season.

Birds don't need a perch on the front of the bird house — a perch is most useful to predators that are trying to steal eggs or young. Although you may appreciate rounded corners on a bird house and a well-sanded exterior, birds prefer rough wood and a natural look.

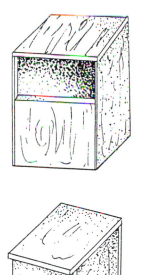

Different styles of nest boxes.

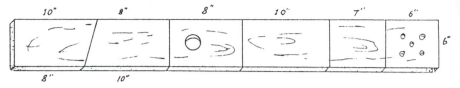

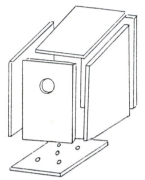

An exploded view of the
construction of a nest box
from a plank of wood.

At the end of the season, clean the nest box out. This helps to
prevent nest parasites from over-wintering, and gives birds a
vacant box for the following spring. Don't disturb the house when
it's in use as you may cause the adults to desert their eggs or young.

There are many different designs for nest boxes, but the most
common and often the most effective is a very simple box that can
be made from a single plank of wood. By altering the inside
dimensions, the size of the hole, and the site where the box is
placed, you should be able to attract a variety of different species.

Here are a few basic dimensions for some common cavity-
nesting species:

	Floor Size	Depth	Hole Diameter	Height
House Wren	10 x 10 cm	15 - 20 cm	2.5 cm	1 - 3 m
Black-capped Chickadee	10 x 10 cm	20 - 25 cm	3 cm	1.5 - 4.5 m
Tree Swallow	12 x 12 cm	15 - 25 cm	4 cm	1.5 - 4.5 cm
Mountain Bluebird	12 x 12 cm	20 - 25 cm	4 cm	1 - 3 m
Northern Flicker	20 x 20 cm	40 - 45 cm	7 cm	2.5 - 6 m

Although House Sparrows and European Starlings will be attracted to next boxes, it is wise to discourage them as they quickly displace native species and drive them from our neighbourhoods.

There are some basic rules to be kept in mind. If the nest box is exposed to full sunlight during the hottest part of the day, the nestlings may die from heat exhaustion, so choose a shaded area, or the northeast side of an exposed tree, post or building. If the box is on a wall, the same will apply — so choose a spot that is shaded by a tree or a climbing plant. Keep the box level or tilted slightly down so that the hole is not exposed to rain. Avoid trees that cats like to climb, or put on an anti-cat barrier at the bottom: an inverted wire cone fixed to the tree about 1.5 metres above the ground usually suffices. There is nothing more upsetting than having the family cat bring you a present of the young birds that you have been watching.

Try to put the nest box in a position that looks as natural as possible and emulates a natural cavity. For your own pleasure, situate it where you can see what is going on from some convenient vantage point.

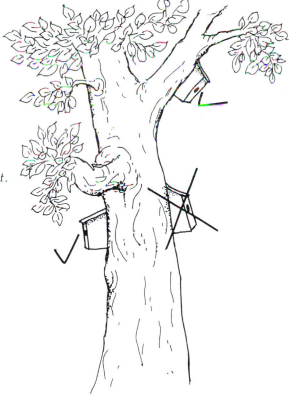

Nest box placement.

109

A BIRD GARDEN

Food, shelter and water are the necessities for all birds at all seasons. A simple bird feeder will bring a variety of seed-eating birds to the garden, but there is little chance of luring insect-eating birds without an appealing environment for them. Even some of the seed-eating species are very shy at the feeder and to attract these birds it is necessary to "think natural" and create some attractive mini-habitats.

It is possible to determine the types of birds that will come to your garden by providing the sort of surroundings that give them shelter, nesting opportunities and food. Flycatchers and other insect-eating birds will be attracted in spring and summer to flower gardens where insects are likely to be abundant. Seed-eating birds will find both shelter and food in the wilder sections of a back yard, where shrubs and weeds combine to provide dense cover and year-round access to food in the form of seeds. A varied garden plot will lure birds where a flawless lawn will not, and a mix of shrubs and taller trees will attract a far greater variety and abundance of birds than a hedge of uniform trees or shrubs. It is

Sapsucker drilling holes for sap.

110

not only berry bushes and fruit trees that provide food; seeds, insects feeding on plants, and water are at least as likely to entice birds.

Birds are also attracted to gardens where there is plenty of shelter in which to rest during the day, or to roost at night, where they can escape from the hottest weather in the summer, and find some protection in the winter. Gardens with mature trees and plenty of shrub cover will be attractive. Some birds also appreciate an area of longer grass and if it is possible to keep an area of the garden as "wild" as you can, it will attract all sorts of creatures, not just birds.

Starling resting on a fence post.

Planting to Attract Birds

Berry Bushes Native shrubs are a principal food source for birds in the wild and will prove a major attraction for birds in the city as well. Although it is possible to transplant shrubs from the wild, this is not a very conservation-minded practice, and many plants do not transplant well. It is preferable try some of the better garden centres, many of which offer a complete range of native shrubs and trees, along with a great deal of good advice.

Among those shrubs that birds find attractive are chokecherry, pincherry, red-osier dogwood, saskatoon, gooseberry, hawthorn, juniper, cranberry and currant.

The mountain ash berries often attract flocks of Cedar Waxwings to visit a garden in winter.

The garden centres may also supply you with a host of other choices in shrubs that birds find equally attractive, including cotoneaster, honeysuckle, huckleberry, raspberry, red and black currant, viburnum and elderberry.

Trees Fruit trees and bushes sometimes provide an unwelcome attraction to birds, as anyone who grows fruit will know. However, some trees produce fruit that is very attractive to birds, but of little or no value to humans. Trees such as the mountain ash are good berry producers and will be visited by American Robins, Bohemian Waxwings, Evening Grosbeaks and other species. The dangling Rowan berries are not easy to reach and such a tree is likely to be visited repeatedly. In consequence, the food — and the entertainment — is likely to last the winter.

Apple and crabapple trees also serve as a major cold-weather food source for birds. They are often picked clean in the early part of the winter, although small crabapples frequently last through until spring. Decorative plum trees may also hold their fruit into the winter months, and can provide a welcome food source.

Water Birds need water throughout the year, and meeting this need may well attract more birds to your garden than will a varied food supply.

A bird bath that is kept unfrozen in the coldest weather will attract many birds. During the summer months, a bird bath can become a busy place, providing endless pleasure for both the birds and the birdwatcher.

Choose or build a bird bath that is not too deep (no more than 7 cm), shelves gradually and is finished in a rough texture so that it is easy for birds to grip. Birds get engrossed in drinking and bathing and when they have wet feathers, they don't fly quite so well. Therefore, if the bath is on or near ground level, make sure that it is situated well away from bushes, so that cats can not approach the bath unseen.

You can keep the water in your bird bath unfrozen during the coldest winters with a small heater available on the market, and you can make the bath particularly attractive to birds in summer by creating a trickly flow or spray of water with a small electric pump.

SEASONS OF BIRD WATCHING

Spring

Although the American Robin is the traditional and much celebrated harbinger of spring, there are a number of birds which may precede it and cheer the lengthening days, including the Western Meadowlark whose song is a clear note of fresh promise.

A few unusual birds will follow, such as the Northern Shrike, which has perhaps wintered a little further south and is moving north again with the increase in daylight. As soon as there is the first sign of break-up and the chance for an edge of water in the shallow ponds, look for Killdeer and Ring-billed Gulls and listen for the haunting call of Canada Geese far overhead. Horned Larks are also among the early arrivals.

And soon, shortly after the robin, the flights of returning migrants will begin in earnest. Late spring, when the trees are just beginning to leaf out and the birds are still easy to spot among the foliage, is an excellent time for bird watching.

Red-tailed Hawk building a nest on same high branches.

A pair of Black-billed Magpies high on a bridge.

Summer

This is the time of nesting birds, and the year-round residents are augmented by scores of species that find the city an ideal nesting area. Identification of birds takes on a diminished importance as their territorial enthusiasm and courtship antics become the centre of attention. For those who have had the foresight to set up nesting boxes or the good fortune to have some of their trees selected as nesting sites, the hours of early summer can be richly occupied in watching as the eggs hatch and the fledglings begin their development.

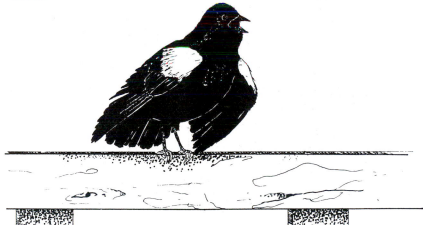

The display of a male Red-winged Blackbird during the mating season.

Fall

From late summer on, the return migration is underway. It is the most likely time to see the largest variety of species. Warblers which flew over the city in the spring now welcome the rest and the food promised by foliage-covered trees. Uncommon birds are likely to be sighted in any back yard and almost certain to be found in those with a dense growth of both shrubs and trees.

Late summer and early fall produce a rich variety of bird life for the further reason that many adults which may have nested outside the city are now free to wander into urban areas in their quest for seeds, insects or berries. The young, which in many species are now independent, will also be foraging much more widely prior to migration.

As the daylight hours diminish, large flocks of waterfowl begin to be seen and heard overhead. Although any watcher is tempted to melancholy at the sight of flocks winging south, it is an ideal time for a birdwatching expedition to a nearby lake or slough to view the marshalling of the flights.

Winter

A number of birds remain and a few even arrive for winter. For those willing to locate a variety of feeders and suet bags around the house, it will be a rare day when no birds arrive. In recent years, winter counts have recorded as many as sixty species in and around Edmonton.

KEEPING BIRD NOTES

Keeping records of the birds you see in your back yard and on excursions will provide you with many hours of pleasure. A daily or weekly checklist of sightings will tell you a great deal about avian visitors to your area. It will furnish a record of how numbers change throughout the seasons and from year to year, and of specific migration times of many species. You will soon know just when to expect your first Western Meadowlark of the spring, or the first Pine Grosbeak of the autumn.

In order to increase your knowledge about individual species, use the birds' behaviour as a clue. Do they "hawk" for insects on a snag on the forest edge, or rustle around for seeds on a deciduous forest floor? Do they like a shrubby canopy that provides continuous shelter, or are they usually seen on tree tops? Build up profiles of individual species, and you'll discover personalities as individual as those of your friends.

Your notes and observations can tell you what birds were common in which years and what parts of your area were particularly good for various species. As well as being of interest to you, this information may make an important contribution to local knowledge by helping ornithologists understand how numbers of birds in your area are changing. This sort of information is often

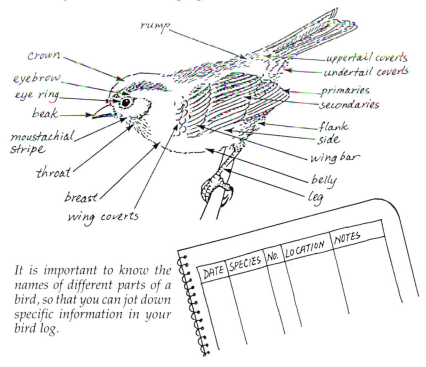

It is important to know the names of different parts of a bird, so that you can jot down specific information in your bird log.

not available when it is needed, and may help to protect your favorite birding spot, should it be threatened with development.

Try to record a clear image of what the bird looked like — a simple line sketch is ideal, and it really doesn't matter how artistic it is! Include as much information as you can about the bird, its plumage characteristics, its bill, leg colour, sounds, and what behaviour the bird exhibited.

You might also want to keep a bird log. This would include the species you saw, how many, where and when (see diagram).

Keep your records in a notebook to avoid losing them. If you intend to take your notebook on hikes, choose one that has a soft waterproof cover; this will allow you to stuff it into a pocket or your pack and it will not disintegrate in the rain. A useful tip: pencils are easier to sketch with, and they write more easily than pen on damp paper.

Another good way to learn more about birds is to join your local natural history or bird society. You will meet many knowledgeable people who will be pleased to teach you what they know about birds and the best places to see them in various areas. Many organizations run field trips to some of the good birdwatching spots and provide the benefit of an expert to help with identification problems. Christmas Bird Counts are a highlight for birdwatchers, regardless of skill level: look for information on these in local papers.

Good birding!

SIGHTING NOTES

DATE _____ TIME _____

LOCATION _____

SPECIES _____ QUANTITY _____

ALTERNATIVE (IF UNCERTAIN) _____

MALE _____ FEMALE _____ IMMATURE _____

HABITAT_____NEST _____

FEEDING PATTERN _____

FLIGHT PATTERN_____

BEHAVIOUR _____

VOICE _____

WARNING CALLS _____

COMMENTS:

SIGHTING NOTES

DATE _____ TIME _____

LOCATION _____

SPECIES _____ QUANTITY _____

ALTERNATIVE (IF UNCERTAIN) _____

MALE _____ FEMALE _____ IMMATURE _____

HABITAT_____ NEST_____

FEEDING PATTERN _____

FLIGHT PATTERN _____

BEHAVIOUR _____

VOICE _____

WARNING CALLS _____

COMMENTS:

SIGHTING NOTES

DATE _____ TIME _____

LOCATION _____

SPECIES _____ QUANTITY _____

ALTERNATIVE (IF UNCERTAIN) _____

MALE _____ FEMALE _____ IMMATURE _____

HABITAT _____ NEST_____

FEEDING PATTERN _____

FLIGHT PATTERN _____

BEHAVIOUR _____

VOICE _____

WARNING CALLS _____

COMMENTS:

SIGHTING NOTES

DATE _____ TIME _____

LOCATION _____

SPECIES _____ QUANTITY _____

ALTERNATIVE (IF UNCERTAIN) _____

MALE _____ FEMALE _____ IMMATURE _____

HABITAT_____ NEST _____

FEEDING PATTERN _____

FLIGHT PATTERN _____

BEHAVIOUR _____

VOICE _____

WARNING CALLS _____

COMMENTS:

SIGHTING NOTES

DATE _____ TIME _____

LOCATION _____

SPECIES _____ QUANTITY _____

ALTERNATIVE (IF UNCERTAIN) _____

MALE _____ FEMALE _____ IMMATURE _____

HABITAT _____ NEST _____

FEEDING PATTERN _____

FLIGHT PATTERN _____

BEHAVIOUR _____

VOICE _____

WARNING CALLS _____

COMMENTS:

RECOMMENDED READING

There are many excellent bird books on the market, among the most useful and informative being:

The Audubon Society Guide to Attracting Birds. Stephen W. Kress. Charles Scribner's Sons. New York. 1985.

The Birder's Handbook - A Field Guide to the Natural History of North American Birds. P. Ehrlich, D. Dobkin, D. Wheye. Simon and Shuster Inc. Toronto. 1988.

The Birds of Alberta. W. Ray Salt and Jim R. Salt. Hurtig Publishers. Edmonton. 1976.

Birds of Canada. W. Earl Godfrey. National Museum of Natural Sciences, National Museums of Canada. Ottawa. 1986. Revised Edition.

Birds of North America: A Guide to Field Identification. Chandler S. Robbins, Bertel Bruun, Herbert S. Zim. Golden Press. New York. Western Publishing Inc. Racine, Wisconsin. 1983.

The Bird Feeder Book. Donald and Lilliam Stokes. Little, Brown and Company. Boston, Toronto. 1987.

The Complete Book of Birdhouse Construction for Woodworkers. Scott D. Campbell. Dover Publications Inc. New York. 1984.

Calgary's Natural Areas: A Popular Guide. Calgary Field Naturalists' Society. P.O. Box 981, Calgary, AB T2P 2R4. 1974.

Field Guide to the Birds of North America. National Geographic Society. 1983.

Inglewood Bird Sanctuary. Dave Elphinstone. Rocky Mountain Books. 1990.

Making Birdhouses and Feeders. Charles R. Self. Sterling Publishing Co. Inc. Two Park Avenue, New York, N.Y. 10016. 1985.

Winging It in Edmonton. Margit Boronkay, Sue Fast, Anita Maloney. The Edmonton Nature Centres' Foundation. 1985.

DIRECTORY OF ALBERTA ORGANIZATIONS

For further information on birdwatching in Alberta, contact:

Alberta Ornithological Records
Committee
Box 981
Calgary AB
T2P 2K4

Alberta Wilderness Association
P.O. Box 6398
Station D
Calgary AB
T2P 2E1

Beaverhill Bird Observatory
P.O. Box 4201
Edmonton AB
T6E 4T2

Beaverhill Lake Nature Centre
Box 30
Tofield AB
T0B 4J0

Bow Valley Naturalists
Box 1693
Banff AB
T0L 0C0

Calgary Field Naturalists
Society
Box 981
Calgary AB
T2P 2K4

Canadian Nature Federation
c/o 8306-158 Street
Edmonton AB
T5R 2C4

Ducks Unlimited
#302 10335-172 St.
Edmonton AB
T5S 1K9

Edmonton Bird Club
Box 4441
Edmonton AB
T6E 4T5

Edmonton Natural History Club
Box 1582
Edmonton AB
T5J 2N9

Federation of Alberta Naturalists
Box 1472
Edmonton AB
T5J 2N5
or 1621-4 Street N.W.
Calgary AB
T2M 2Z1

Fish Creek Provincial Park
Box 2780
Calgary AB
T2P 0Y8

Inglewood Bird Sanctuary
c/o The City of Calgary
Parks and Recreation Department
Box 2100
Station M
Calgary AB
T2P 2M5

John Janzen Nature Centre
P.O. Box 2359
Edmonton AB
T5J 2R7

Peace Parkland Naturalists Club
c/o Glen Rogers
9902-101 Street
Grand Prairie AB
T8V 2P5

Red Deer River Naturalists
Box 785
Red Deer AB
T4N 5H2

Rocky Mountain House Bird Club
Box 764
Rocky Mountain House AB
T0M 1T0

INDEX TO BIRDS

ABOUT THE AUTHOR

ROBIN BOVEY is a writer, photographer, and editor who lives in Edmonton. Formerly with the Nature Conservancy Council in the United Kingdom, he recently co-authored *Mosses, Lichens and Ferns of Northwest North America*, with Dale Vitt and Janet Marsh. His many interests include drama, environmental awareness, and natural history projects.

ABOUT THE ILLUSTRATOR

EWA PLUCIENNIK was born and raised in Opole, Silesia, Poland, and has been living in Alberta for approximately three years. Specializing in water colour and oil paintings, she recently completed a series of illustrations for *Dinosaurs of the West*, by Ron Stewart.